ENGLAND CRICKET LEGENDS
SINCE 1946

DEAN P. HAYES
Foreword by FRED TITMUS

SUTTON PUBLISHING

Sutton Publishing Limited
Phoenix Mill · Thrupp · Stroud
Gloucestershire · GL5 2BU

First published 2002

Title page photograph: Darren Gough. (LEP)

British Library Cataloguing in Publication Data
A catalogue record for this book is available from the British Library.

ISBN 0-7509-2968-5

Typeset in 10.5/13.5 Photina.
Typesetting and origination by
Sutton Publishing Limited.
Printed and bound in England by
J.H. Haynes & Co. Ltd, Sparkford.

Picture Credits

The majority of the images in this book have been kindly provided by the *Lancashire Evening Post* (LEP), the *Manchester Evening News* (MEN), the *Evening Standard* (ES) and the *Northampton Chronicle and Echo* (NCE). The rest are from the author's own collection.

Photos LEP

Contents

Foreword by Fred Titmus   4
Introduction   5

THE LEGENDS

Dennis Amiss

John Edrich

Peter May

Geoff Arnold

John Emburey

Chris Old

Mike Atherton

Godfrey Evans

Geoff Pullar

Trevor Bailey

Keith Fletcher

Derek Randall

Ken Barrington

Angus Fraser

Tim Robinson

Alec Bedser

Mike Gatting

Jack Russell

Ian Botham

Graham Gooch

Mike Smith

Geoff Boycott

Darren Gough

Robin Smith

Mike Brearley

David Gower

John Snow

Chris Broad

Tom Graveney

Brian Statham

Andy Caddick

Tony Greig

David Steele

Brian Close

Graeme Hick

Alec Stewart

Denis Compton

Nasser Hussain

Bob Taylor

Dominic Cork

Len Hutton

Graham Thorpe

Colin Cowdrey

Ray Illingworth

Fred Titmus

Mike Denness

Alan Knott

Fred Trueman

Ted Dexter

Jim Laker

Frank Tyson

Graham Dilley

Allan Lamb

Derek Underwood

Basil D'Oliveira

Tony Lock

Cyril Washbrook

Bill Edrich

Devon Malcolm

Bob Willis

Statistics   126

Foreword

Fred Titmus, Middlesex and England

This book gives a valuable insight into England's post-war Test match history through the portrayal of sixty of the personalities who have played for their country during this period. Through the eyes of the individuals concerned, Dean Hayes relives some of the most exciting moments of Test cricket, from the glorious summer of 1947 to England's recent exploits on the sub-continent, including 'Laker's match', 'Botham's Ashes', and much much more!

I made my Test debut against South Africa at Lord's way back in 1955 and though I was extremely proud and delighted to have been selected, I was also very surprised as a certain gentleman by the name of Jim Laker was still on the scene. In 1962/3 on my first tour of Australia, I was third in line

behind Allen and Illingworth in the spin bowling department, yet played all five Tests. At Sydney I produced my best-ever bowling figures at Test level, taking 7 for 79, yet the bowling performance that gave me the greatest pleasure came two years later against India at Kanpur when I took 6 for 73 off 60 overs.

Sadly the boating accident in the Caribbean curtailed my Test career for a good number of years, until in 1974/5 I was recalled for my third tour 'Down Under'. Facing the pace of Lillee and Thomson was quite hair-raising, for in those days there were no helmets. As I strode to the wicket my thoughts were with my wife and young daughter in the stand, but thankfully I'd been around long enough to know which way to sway and when.

I've been lucky enough to play in 53 Tests for England alongside some of the country's greatest players, household names such as Compton, Cowdrey, Lock, May, Statham and Trueman to name just a few. Of all the great Test players I have played against, one stands out above all the others – Gary Sobers, the complete cricketer.

When my playing days were over, I became a Test selector. It was something I'd always wanted to do. I like to think that Brian Bolus and I started a new trend by watching county cricket day in, day out as we sought to find new talent. Nowadays, I don't watch as much cricket, though I do attend the Lord's Test and look forward to the day when England are back on top of the cricket world.

This book, I am sure, will give all followers of English cricket many hours of happy reading, as well as providing an invaluable work of reference.

Introduction

Every cricket follower, no matter what his age, fancies himself as a selector. Some may be more dogmatic than others, some more realistic, but I am sure each and every one has at some time indulged himself in picking an England team to beat the choice of the selectors or the all-conquering Australians.

No doubt my choice of sixty players from the 317 to have played for England in the post-war years will not meet with universal approval. I have omitted players reluctantly and included others tentatively. It may ease some readers' minds if I add a list of regretted omissions. There is no place for Jim Parks, an entertaining free-flowing stroke-maker, Peter Parfitt who averaged over 40 in his 37 Tests or Neil Foster, whose remarkable 11-wicket haul against India in Madras was a match-winning performance. Perhaps two of the inclusions call for an explanation but Devon Malcolm's 9 for 57 against South Africa at The Oval in 1994 and David Steele's heroic displays against Australia in 1975 in my opinion led to their deserved inclusion in this collection of sixty post-war heroes while Graeme Hick is the author's son's favourite player of all-time!

I hope you enjoy this book and enjoy equally arguing and disagreeing with the selections made.

Dean Hayes
Pembrokeshire
April 2002

Photos LEP

Dennis Amiss

Born: 7 April 1943, Harborne, Birmingham

- He scored 262 not out, hitting a six and 40 fours against West Indies at Kingston in 1973/4.
- His aggregate of 1,379 runs in 1974 was just two short of Bobby Simpson's record (subsequently beaten).
- He holds the Warwickshire records for most runs (35,146) and hundreds(78).
- He scored 1,000 runs in each of 23 consecutive seasons (1965–87), including 2,000 three times.

A PHLEGMATIC, determined opening batsman, Dennis Amiss was a patient accumulator of runs with massive powers of concentration and an insatiable appetite for large scores. The Warwickshire batsman actually made his first appearance at Edgbaston while still only 14, playing at the end of the season in a final of the Docker Shield, the biggest schools

LEP

league competition in the country. Then a diminutive bustling all-rounder, batting right-handed but bowling a brisk medium-pace left arm 'seam up', he was told to come back when he was 15. He was there at the Thwaites Gates within minutes of leaving school and was offered an engagement.

Though he made his Warwickshire debut in 1960 at the age of 17 it was not until 1965 that he established himself as a regular member of the county side, ending the season as Warwickshire's leading scorer with 1,433 runs. By now he had given up any serious aspirations as a bowler on medical advice, not wishing to aggravate earlier back troubles which undoubtedly delayed his development as a batsman.

The following year he was picked for England for the fifth Test against the West Indies at The Oval – a memorable game in which Tom Graveney and John Murray hit hundreds and Ken Higgs and John Snow put on 128 for the last wicket. Amiss scored 17 before being leg-before wicket to Wes Hall. England won by an innings, so his performance was restricted to one knock, but it was the first step up a long hill which he was finally to scale with courage, determination and distinction. After a rocky beginning – 348 runs at an average of 18.31 in his first 12 Tests – Amiss amassed over 2,000 runs at an average of 71.33 with eight hundreds in the next 20 matches. It took Amiss a long time to establish a regular place in the England team, only doing so towards the end of the 1972/3 tour of India and Pakistan, after he had reached his first Test century in his thirteenth Test at Lahore.

From 1972 to late 1974 he was England's outstanding run-getter, scoring 1,379 runs in a single year – just two runs short of Bobby Simpson's record Test aggregate in a calendar year. The total included his marathon match-saving career best innings of 262 not out at Sabina Park, Kingston. Had Bob Willis not survived for almost an hour during an unbroken last-wicket partnership, Amiss would

LEP

have become only the fourth to carry his bat through a completed innings for England and his would have been the highest such score in Tests. Another century followed at Georgetown, pursued by scores of 188 against India and 193 against Pakistan in the home series.

He followed this run of high scores with a series of depressing failures. In 1974/5 he was completely overwhelmed by the formidable Australian pace attack and thereafter lost his wicket to Dennis Lillee on numerous occasions, suffering several blows to the head. But he did manage a remarkable double century against a rampant Michael Holding at The Oval in 1976 and enjoyed a successful tour of India where he made 179 in the first Test at Delhi before joining the Packer bandwagon. This effectively ended his Test career.

To this point, the image of Dennis Amiss was one of a loyal and dedicated professional cricketer – he had received a record declared benefit from Warwickshire – but temporary bitterness was quickly forgotten. He treated Warwickshire followers to another decade of fine batting, scoring 35,146 runs for the county – his confidence reinforced by protective headgear which he was the first to market in Britain. Made an MBE for his services to cricket, Dennis Amiss is still at Edgbaston as Warwickshire's much respected Chief Executive.

Geoff Arnold

Born: 3 September 1944, Earlsfield, Surrey

- He is the only bowler to have taken a wicket with the first ball of a Test on two occasions.
- He performed the hat trick for Surrey v Leicestershire at Grace Road in 1974.

TEST CAREER

BATTING

M	34
I	46
NO	11
Runs	421
HSc	59
Av	12.02
100	–
50	1

BOWLING

Runs	3,254
Wkts	115
Av	28.29
Best	6-45
5w	6
10w	–
Ct	9
St	–

GEOFFREY GRAHAM ARNOLD – "Orse" to his Surrey team-mates, which could have been a tribute to his capacity for work as well as to his parents' choice of initials – was a late developer in cricket. After joining Surrey in 1962 and having his first game the following summer, he made sufficient progress to be chosen for the England Under-25 team to tour Pakistan in 1966/7. In a Zone match there, he was run out for 71. Thereby hangs a tale. There had been words between him, the bowler, and Saeed Ahmed, the batsman. When it was his turn to bat, Arnold backed up too enthusiastically, so Saeed took the bails off. Arnold asked if this was a warning and the answer was 'No, I'm appealing.' So Arnold had to go.

In 1967, the day after he heard he had won his first cap against Pakistan, he took 8 for 41 against Gloucestershire – his best-ever figures with the ball. In only his second Test match Arnold scored 59 and took 5 for 58 at The Oval – further proof that given the opportunity, he could well have been a genuine all-rounder.

Misfortune in the shape of injuries kept him back for the next few years. He missed most of 1968 because of a cartilage operation, played in only one Test in 1969 and did not reach his full potential until 1971 when he took 75 wickets at 16.28 runs apiece to head the national bowling averages and help Surrey win the County Championship.

In the 1971 Tests he got no further than twelfth man but the arrival of the 1972 Australians gave him his big chance. In the first Test at Old Trafford in conditions ideal for swing and seam bowling he had Keith Stackpole missed at slip off one ball, missed again in the slips off the next (off which Stackpole scored a single) and had Bruce Francis missed at slip off the next – an unprecedented feat of unrewarded accuracy! A hamstring injury kept him out of the Lord's Test but by the end of 1972 he was the acknowledged fast-medium complement to the speed of John Snow.

In the five series against Australia in 1972, in India and Pakistan in 1972/3 and against New Zealand in 1973 Arnold took 64 wickets in only 16 matches – proof that he had reached the top as a leading exponent of the art of new-ball bowling. During that spell Arnold produced his best bowling figures in a Test match, 6 for 45 against India at Delhi on a pitch normally unfriendly to a bowler of his type.

He had originally received tips from Peter Loader on how to hold the ball so that on pitching it would move either way dependent on the angle at which the seam hit the ground. Alec Bedser taught him how to bowl the unplayable ball which swings into the batsman and then leaves him off the pitch – Bedser's famous leg-cutter.

Though Arnold came close to performing the hat trick while playing for Surrey 2nd XI against Essex, having future West Indian all-rounder Keith Boyce dropped at slip after taking two wickets in two balls, he finally achieved the feat against Leicestershire at Grace Road in 1974. Arnold left Surrey in 1978 to play for Sussex, having taken 745 first-class wickets at 19.94 runs apiece. He spent five years on the south coast before returning to The Oval as Surrey's coach.

Arnold was a bundle of nerves before a big match but give him the new ball and all trace of those nerves vanished as he concentrated on thinking out his opponent. He loved bowling and would go on all day if asked – a great asset to his captain.

LEP

Mike Atherton

Born: 23 March 1968, Failsworth, Manchester

- He was voted Young Cricketer of the Year and was one of *Wisden*'s Five Cricketers of the Year in 1990.
- He captained England in 53 of his 115 Tests – an England record.
- He scored 185 not out v South Africa at Johannesburg in November 1995.
- He was made an OBE in 1997.
- He scored 1,000 runs in a season on seven occasions with a highest score of 268 not out v Glamorgan at Blackpool in 1999.

TEST CAREER

BATTING

M	115
I	212
NO	7
Runs	7,728
HSc	185*
Av	37.69
100	16
50	46

BOWLING

Runs	302
Wkts	2
Av	151.00
Best	1-20
5w	–
10w	–
Ct	83
St	–

MICHAEL ATHERTON captained England a record 53 times and played in 63 consecutive Tests between 1993 and 1998. He was troubled by a back injury for much of his international career, but his dogged determination and a successful training schedule gave him a longer Test career than he might have expected.

Educated at Manchester Grammar School and Cambridge University, where he excelled as a player and captain, Mike Atherton made his Test debut at 21 and impressed with his technique, temperament and composure at the crease. At Manchester Grammar School, he had smashed

batting records and at the age of 16 captained the England Under-19s, which reinforced the suspicion at the time that he would one day lead England through the Long Room at Lord's. His career choice was confirmed after an unbeaten 73 as a freshman for Cambridge University against a rampant Essex attack. Cambridge had been reduced to 20 for 7 before Atherton worked his miracle. Captain of Cambridge, where he hit three centuries and a highest of 151 against Middlesex at Fenner's, he also led the Combined Universities on their enterprising giant-killing run in the 1989 Benson & Hedges Cup.

He made his Lancashire debut against Warwickshire in 1987, a summer in which he scored 1,183 first-class runs to become the first batsman since Sussex's Paul Parker in 1976 to make over 1,000 runs in a debut season. He scored his maiden century for Lancashire against Sussex at Hove in 1988 when he made an unbeaten 152. The following summer he was awarded his county cap and selected to play for England in two Tests against Australia, scoring 47 at Trent Bridge. At the end of the season he was selected as vice-captain for the England 'A' team tour to Kenya and Zimbabwe, where his

LEP

contribution to planning and strategy confirmed him as a ready-made successor to Graham Gooch as England captain.

Atherton continued to score runs by the ton for Lancashire and he trod in some famous footprints at Trent Bridge in June 1990 to become, at 22, the youngest Englishman to make a Test hundred since the 21-year-old David Gower achieved the feat in India in 1978. That summer was also his first full season with Lancashire. No one at Old Trafford did more to lead Lancashire's assault on the Britannic Championship, Benson & Hedges Cup and Refuge Assurance League, Atherton ending the campaign with 1,170 runs at an average of 78.00.

In 1993 Atherton followed Percy Chapman, Gubby Allen, Peter May, Ted Dexter, Mike Brearley and others to the tenancy of the captain's locker in the England dressing-room. Atherton's 'flawless' technique was still vulnerable against bowling of the highest class though his nimble footwork took him into positions to play shots all round the wicket, a priceless gift for an opening batsman hoping not to get bogged down against tight bowling. He was often the springboard for an England innings but was not always supported by his colleagues in terms of building decent totals.

Atherton made his 100th Test appearance against the West Indies at Old Trafford in the summer of 2000, reaching the milestone in the same match as Alec Stewart. His mammoth innings of 185 not out against South Africa in the second Test at Johannesburg in November 1995 was his highest Test score.

Made an OBE in 1997, Michael Atherton returned from successful winter tours to Pakistan and Sri Lanka to play in his last Ashes series in the summer of 2001 before announcing his decision to retire from first-class cricket.

LEP

Trevor Bailey

Born: 3 December 1923, Westcliff-on-Sea, Essex

- He took a wicket with his eighth ball in Test cricket and returned a six-wicket analysis in his first innings.
- He took all ten Lancashire wickets for 90 at Clacton in 1949.
- He performed the hat trick for Essex v Glamorgan at Newport in 1950 and claimed seven wickets in 29 balls in the return fixture at Brentwood.
- He scored 50 in 357 minutes v Australia at Brisbane – still the slowest recorded fifty in first-class cricket!
- He passed 1,000 runs 17 times with a best of 2,011 in 1959.
- He did the double on eight occasions – a total exceeded only by W. Rhodes, G.H. Hirst, V.W.C. Jupp and W.E. Astill.

TEST CAREER

BATTING

M	61
I	91
NO	14
Runs	2,290
HSc	134*
Av	29.74
100	1
50	10

BOWLING

Runs	3,856
Wkts	132
Av	29.21
Best	7-34
5w	5
10w	1
Ct	32
St	–

TREVOR BAILEY played his first game for Essex during the war years, impressing immediately in his opening game with 4 for 36, including three wickets in his first over. He also represented several sides at Lord's including an England XI against a West Indian XI, and the British Empire XI when on leave from the Royal Marines.

After the war, Bailey attended Cambridge University and was only able to appear for Essex at the end of term. However, in only his second season he hit a superb 205 against Sussex at Eastbourne – this was to be his highest score in first-class cricket.

Throughout the cricketing world Trevor Bailey is 'The Boil'. This unusual nickname originated from a visit to Switzerland in the winter of 1947/8 with the Cambridge University soccer team. The Swiss announcer was having difficulty with the longer names in the Cambridge XI and announced that 'Boiley' would play at outside-right. This was subsequently abbreviated to 'The Boil' and its adoption by Freddie Brown on the Australian tour of 1950/1 ensured its permanency.

At the beginning of the 1948 season it was decided to offer Bailey the position of assistant-secretary at Essex. This enabled him to devote all his time to playing first-class cricket after coming down from Cambridge. In 1949 every possible distinction came to Bailey. He was selected by the MCC for its match against New Zealand and then played in four successive Test matches. During this four-match series he had scores of 93 and 72 not out and bowling figures of 6 for 84 and 6 for 118 – which he took in his first Test. He achieved the double, scoring 1,380 runs and capturing 130 wickets in 1949, and in the match against Lancashire at Clacton, took all ten wickets in the red rose county's first innings for 90 runs. He was only the second Essex bowler to accomplish this feat, the other being Henry Pickett. Not surprisingly he was chosen as one of *Wisden*'s Five Cricketers of the Year. In 1950 he performed the hat trick against Glamorgan at Newport while in the return at Brentwood, he took 7 for 0 in 29 balls.

When injuries began to restrict his appearances for Essex, he managed to gain an FA Amateur Cup Winner's medal while playing for Walthamstow Avenue against Leyton.

In 1953 he was appointed Essex's vice-captain, a position he was to hold until he took over as captain from Doug Insole. During the Test series against Australia his innings of 71 in the fifth-wicket partnership of 163 with Willie Watson saved the series for England. In the winter tour to the West Indies he turned in his best bowling figures in Test cricket, taking 7 for 34 at Kingston.

Bailey had a reputation for some dour performances with the bat, Neville Cardus saying that he 'stonewalled with passion'. In 1955 he hit a hundred before lunch against Nottinghamshire at Southend and over the next couple of seasons he topped Essex's batting and bowling averages. In 1957 in the Lord's Test match against the West Indies he took 7 for 44 in 21 overs. It was his fiftieth Test match and his victims included Walcott, Weekes and Worrell. In 1959 Bailey scored 2,011 runs and took 100 wickets; it was the first time such a feat had been performed by an Essex player. Bailey began the 1961 season as Essex captain, a natural successor to Doug Insole who had resigned owing to business commitments. He led by example, achieving the double for the seventh time and repeating the feat the following season but injuries then restricted his appearances and in 1967 he decided to retire.

Without doubt the finest all-round cricketer ever to play for Essex, Trevor Bailey went on to become an important member of the BBC's radio commentary team.

ES

Ken Barrington

Born: 24 November 1930, Reading, Berkshire
Died: 14 May 1981, Needham's Point, Bridgetown

- In the match against India at Bombay on the 1961/2 tour he batted for over nine hours without being dismissed.
- He ended that series with the record aggregate of 594 runs at an average of 99.00.
- He was the second batsman after J. Darling (1897/8) to complete 100 in England v Australia Tests with a six.
- His score of 256 against Australia in 1964 remains England's highest at Old Trafford and his batting time of 683 minutes is the second-longest first-class innings by an Englishman.

TEST CAREER	
BATTING	
M	82
I	131
NO	15
Runs	6,806
HSc	256
Av	58.67
100	20
50	35
BOWLING	
Runs	1,300
Wkts	29
Av	44.82
Best	3-4
5w	–
10w	–
Ct	58
St	–

KEN BARRINGTON was one of the most prolific post-war batsmen in world cricket until a heart attack in October 1968 ended his first-class career shortly before his 39th birthday.

It was as a leg-spinner that Barrington was recommended to Surrey in 1947. He had become assistant groundsman to the Reading club for which he was taking many wickets, and at the age of 16 he was invited to play for the Surrey Colts. He became a professional in 1948 but had to do National Service and it was 1951 before his promise as a batsman became obvious. Under the coaching of Andrew Sandham he soon began to make runs in the Minor Counties competition. He first played for Surrey in a first-class match in 1953 and developed so quickly in 1954 that he played in his first Test match the following year. Perhaps he had come up a little too swiftly, for after his two Tests at Lord's and Headingley against South Africa in 1955, he did not play Test cricket for four years.

Though he had poor seasons in 1956 and 1957, he had the advantage of playing in a strong confident side – this was during Surrey's seven-year reign as champions. He also had the opportunity to watch Peter May, considered the best batsman in the world at close quarters at that time. By 1959, which he began by making a hundred in each innings against Warwickshire, he was a welcome sight for selectors looking for new blood after England's 4–0 defeat in Australia the previous winter.

Thus his Test career was resumed and in the years that followed he made 20 centuries, including at least two against each of England's opponents, and 6,806 runs, a number surpassed at the time of his retirement only by Hammond, Cowdrey, Bradman and Hutton. His first two hundreds were made during the 1959/60 tour of the West Indies and for some years he made most runs on overseas wickets in India, Pakistan and Australia. Strangely, too, he developed a humorous presence on the field with his skill in clowning and mime which communicated itself more easily to overseas crowds than it ever did in England.

By now he had changed his stance to face more towards the bowler. Thus he was mainly an on-side player and a fine cutter but could hit the ball off the front foot on the off-side. His technique, though not strictly from the text-book, was less controversial than his approach to batting. It was generally thought that for a player of his run-making capacity, he scored too slowly. He was too good a batsman, it was felt, to submit to a bowler as readily as he sometimes appeared to do and the fact that he had periods of fluency in most innings strengthened this belief. He would often come in and make 30 runs in reasonable time before slowing down. Several times in Test matches he suddenly emerged from a period of inactivity to reach his hundred with a perfectly struck six. On one famous occasion in Melbourne he made the fastest Test hundred of the year by an Englishman – in 122 balls – and played as boldly and as well as anyone could have asked.

It was not until 1964 that he made his first Test hundred in England but characteristically when it came it was extended to 256 in the marathon innings at Old Trafford with which England answered Australia's 656 and Bobby Simpson's 311. He was then dropped by the England selectors in 1965 after taking what was considered an excessive time to score 137 against New Zealand, but this was a passing interlude in a career for Surrey and England which though seldom spectacular, was immensely productive.

When he retired Barrington became a popular manager or coach on England tours and he was assistant-manager on the tour of the West Indies in 1980/1 when he suffered a second heart attack and died during the Test match at Bridgetown, Barbados.

LEP

Alec Bedser

Born: 4 July 1918, Reading, Berkshire

- He was the first bowler to take 200 wickets for England.
- He exceeded 100 wickets in a season on 11 occasions, including 150 twice.
- He performed the hat trick for Surrey v Essex at The Oval in 1953.
- In the Trent Bridge Test match of 1953 against Australia, Bedser produced a match analysis of 14 for 99 which remains the Test record for Nottingham and was the best by an England bowler since 1934.
- In the Test match against Australia at Lord's in 1948 Bedser dismissed Don Bradman for the fifth time in successive innings.

ALEC BEDSER was a tireless bowler who wore the three lions with pride and would willingly run through a brick wall for his team and country. He was a huge man whose best years were probably spent in the Royal Air Force in the Second World War but who was so dedicated and skilful as a fast-medium exponent that from the time Test cricket resumed after the hostilities he was England's chief strike weapon and remained so through 14 Test series. In fact, Bedser played in every post-war Ashes match until he was left out of the second Test in Australia in 1954/5. He bowed out as the greatest Test wicket-taker up to that time with 236 victims in 51 matches for England at an average of 24.89.

He practised his craft for hour after hour in the nets, putting a white handkerchief on the spot of ideal line and length and hitting the mark almost every time. Bedser was so accurate that despite his lively pace he preferred his wicket-keepers – Godfrey Evans and Arthur McIntyre – to stand up to the stumps for him.

He joined Surrey with his twin brother Eric in 1938 and made his first-class debut against Oxford University in 1939. It was not until after the war that he played his first Test against India, taking 7 for 49 at Lord's. In the second Test at Old Trafford he took 7 for 52 after Lancashire's Dick Pollard had taken 5 for 24 in the first innings. Though he struggled through his first Australian summer later that year, he was back to his best against New Zealand on the way home and retained his place for the visit of South Africa in 1947. That summer he hit his best first-class score of 126 for Surrey against Somerset.

By the time England toured Australia in 1950/1, Bedser was 32 with several arduous series and moderate returns behind him, but in a losing rubber he managed 30 wickets at 16.06 in a remarkable display of consistency. In five matches against the 1951 South African tourists he repeated his Australian success with 30 wickets at 17.23 including 7 for 58 at Old Trafford.

The arrival of Fred Trueman in 1952 told Bedser that his remaining time at the top was short, yet he took 20 wickets at 13.95 against the Indian tourists, beguiling all those who were still standing after Trueman's full frontal assaults. That same year he took 8 for 18 bowling for Surrey against Nottinghamshire at The Oval.

In 1953 Bedser, at the age of 35, broke Maurice Tate's Ashes record with 39 Australian wickets at just 17.48 apiece. At Trent Bridge Bedser followed 7 for 55 in the first innings with his best Test figures of 7 for 44 in the second and in the same season at The Oval he took another 8 for 18 for Surrey against Warwickshire. He took 10 cheap wickets against Pakistan the following summer but the Test debut of Frank Tyson spelled his doom and he played his last match at this level against South Africa at Old Trafford in 1955 as the Springboks won with minutes to spare.

Bedser, a major figure along with Peter Loader in Surrey's remarkable run of County Championships between 1952 and 1958, took 1,924 wickets at 20.41 runs apiece.

A successful businessman, he still made time after his retirement as a player to serve on committees and to become an England selector from 1962. He has been manager and assistant manager on Test tours abroad and in 1969 began a record term as Chairman of Selectors, which lasted until 1982 when Peter May took over.

ES

Ian Botham

Born: 24 November 1955, Heswall, Cheshire

- He scored 1,000 runs and took 100 wickets by his 21st Test – two matches fewer than M.H. Mankad's world record.
- He was the first to score 100 and take eight wickets in an innings of the same Test; his analysis, which included a spell of 6 for 8 in 53 balls, remains the record for Tests at Lord's and for England v Pakistan.
- In the match against India at Bombay in 1979/80 he became the first player to score 100 and take ten wickets in a Test.
- Against Australia at Edgbaston in 1981 he took 5 for 1 in 28 balls.
- In the match against Pakistan in 1983/4 he made the last of 65 consecutive Test appearances to equal Alan Knott's England record.
- In the match against New Zealand at The Oval in 1986 he surpassed Dennis Lillee's world record of 355 Test wickets.
- He hit ten sixes and scored 100 in 52 minutes off 56 balls for Somerset v Warwickshire at Taunton in 1982.
- He performed the hat trick for MCC v Middlesex at Lord's in 1978.

TEST CAREER

BATTING

M	102
I	161
NO	6
Runs	5,200
HSc	208
Av	33.54
100	14
50	22

BOWLING

Runs	10,878
Wkts	383
Av	28.40
Best	8-34
5w	27
10w	4
Ct	120
St	–

IAN BOTHAM is one of the greatest cricketers the world has seen. It is a measure of his stature that although he became the most prolific Test wicket-taker in history, he is likely to be remembered for his batting.

Botham was certainly not free of criticism during his career. He was involved in court cases and frequently offended the cricketing authorities. There were times when he was accused of having a care-free attitude, others when he was called domineering. However, throughout the 1980s Botham was the man who could turn Test matches on his own, the man whose entry to bat was enough to excite crowds to expectancy, the most charismatic cricketer of all.

He made his debut for Somerset in 1974 and after four first-class appearances really showed his mettle in a Benson & Hedges match against Hampshire at Taunton. Somerset faced a total of 182 as the 18-year-old Botham walked to the wicket with the home side on 113 for 7. Soon the score was 113 for 8, with 70 needed in 15 overs. Andy Roberts, the West Indian fast bowler, hit Botham in the face – he was to lose four teeth – but he battled on and saw his side home with an unbeaten 45. The Somerset crowd had seen the rise of a new star.

In 1977 the Test call-up came in the third Test against the touring Australians. Botham's first wicket was Greg Chappell; he finished the first innings with 5 for 74.

In the winter he scored his first Test century against New Zealand and by the end of 1978, during which he hit Pakistan with two centuries, he had produced his best Test analysis of 8 for 34 and had taken 24 wickets against New Zealand. He was the hottest property in cricket.

In 1979 Botham passed 1,000 runs and 100 Test wickets in his 21st Test. In February 1980 in Bombay in India's Golden Jubilee Test he scored 114 and took 13 wickets – the first player to score a century and take ten or more wickets in a Test.

Botham took over the England captaincy in 1980 for the visit of the West Indies. By his standards he had a poor series followed by a poor Centenary Test and then a bad tour of the West Indies where he wasn't helped by the sad death of assistant manager Ken Barrington with whom he shared a birthday and mutual respect. After two matches of the 1981 Ashes series Botham resigned the captaincy. The next Test was one of the most amazing in history. Botham's all-round performance was one of the greatest ever seen. With the ball he took 6 for 95 and with the bat he scored 50 and the match-

LEP

winning 149 not out. The series continued with Botham in similar form: a match-winning 5 for 11 at Edgbaston and a superb 118 at Old Trafford.

In the first Test of the winter tour of India he became the third player after Benaud and Sobers to score 2,000 Test runs and take 200 Test wickets. Though a knee injury ended a run of 65 consecutive Tests for England, he returned for the 1984 series against the West Indies, becoming the first player to complete the double of 3,000 Test runs and 300 Test wickets.

In 1986 he achieved his greatest statistical feat in becoming the leading wicket-taker in Test cricket when he passed Dennis Lillee's total of 355. Botham's figures for Somerset were usually less impressive than his Test figures and after a well-publicised row, following the county's sacking of his friends Viv Richards and Joel Garner, he joined Worcestershire, whom he helped win the Championship in 1988 and 1989. He ended his career with Durham.

It was inevitable that a man of Botham's temperament and ability would attract headlines – he shoots, has flown with the Red Devils aerobatic team, crashed Saab cars and played League football for Scunthorpe United! He has also walked from John O'Groats to Lands End for charity and made a trip over the Alps with elephants. Few cricketers have given more pleasure than Ian Botham.

Geoff Boycott

Born: 21 October 1940, Fitzwilliam, Yorkshire

- In the Headingley Test of 1967 he scored 246 not out – the highest score in England v India Tests. He was excluded from the next Test as a disciplinary measure after spending almost ten hours at the crease!
- He was the first player to score his 100th first-class hundred in a Test against Australia. It came at Headingley in 1977, a match in which he became the fourth England player to be on the field for an entire Test.
- He scored 100 on each of England's major Test grounds.
- He became the fourth man to carry his bat through a completed England innings and the first to do so without scoring 100.
- In December 1981 Boycott passed Gary Sobers's world Test record of 8,032 runs.
- He is the only batsman to average 100 in an English first-class season twice: 2,045 at 100.12 in 1971 and 1,538 at 102.53 in 1979.
- He exceeded 1,000 runs in a home season 23 times (plus three overseas), including 2,000 three times.
- His first-class aggregate of 48,426 runs and 151 hundreds are the eighth and ninth highest respectively.

TEST CAREER

BATTING

M	108
I	193
NO	23
Runs	8,114
HSc	246*
Av	47.72
100	22
50	42

BOWLING

Runs	382
Wkts	7
Av	54.57
Best	3-47
5w	–
10w	–
Ct	44
St	–

GEOFFREY BOYCOTT was one of the most controversial cricketers of modern times. No batsman ever compiled runs in a more single-minded and dedicated manner.

At first sight he was not obviously a batsman of the highest class, but his performances allowed no argument – 1,778 runs in his first full season and 2,110 runs in 1964. After his leap to fame, however, he had some difficult periods and at the end of the 1969 season it seemed his career was not fulfilling its immense early promise. In 1967 he made 246 not out against India at Headingley but spent nearly six

hours over the first 100. The selectors had previously called for a positive approach to batting and this flagrant disregard for their requirements and the fact that it was not warranted by the state of the match meant Boycott was dropped for the next Test. The 1970/1 season in Australia, however, was a personal triumph. His 657 Test runs at an average of 93.85 were instrumental in helping England to regain the Ashes.

In 1974 he voluntarily withdrew from Test cricket, declining to tour Australia in 1974/5, and did not return to Tests until the summer of 1977. Having recovered his personal poise – and having rejected an offer to sign a Packer contract – Boycott announced that he was available for England again. His comeback was dour and nerve-wracking but triumphant, for he made 107 and 80 not out. With his confidence high he made an even more emotional century in the next Test in front of his home crowd at Headingley and his 191 happened to be his 100th first-class century. More ups and downs lay ahead. During the winter tour he succeeded to the English captaincy when Mike Brearley suffered a broken forearm but after averaging

82.25 against Pakistan he had the galling experience of leading England in their first defeat by New Zealand. He also, not for the first time, found himself the centre of controversy over the way he captained and batted for Yorkshire.

The responsibility on his shoulders had frequently been great – his ability to play one long innings after another was desperately needed, particularly by the weak-batting Yorkshire side, whose captaincy he took over in 1971. It was no coincidence that in his first year in charge he averaged over 100. However, in 1978 the Yorkshire Committee relieved Boycott of the captaincy and gave it to John Hampshire. A pro-Boycott Reform Group was set up and challenged the Committee, at first unsuccessfully. In 1983 came a further blow to his pride. He had been granted a benefit for 1984 but the Committee in fact sacked him after the 1983 season to end the 'rancour and controversy of recent years'. This time the pro-Boycott group held a special meeting and won votes of no confidence in the Committee which subsequently resigned. Boycott himself stood in the new elections and was voted on to the Committee.

During the 1981/2 tour of India he passed Gary Sobers's record aggregate of runs in Test cricket. Soon after his return to England he announced that he was to take part in a 'rebel' tour of South Africa. Like the other England Test players who took part in this tour he was banned from Tests for three years. When the ban was lifted in 1985 Boycott found that competition for England places was fierce and he wasn't selected again. His Yorkshire career ended in 1986, although there were doubtless many more runs left in him. Other counties made enquiries but Boycott became a television commentator.

He was controversial to the end but always insisted his figures spoke for him. His critics claimed that the context was as important as the figures but nobody can take away from him his career average of 56.83, his 8,114 Test runs, once the highest in the world, or his two averages of over 100 in a season, which still amount to a unique achievement.

LEP

Mike Brearley

Born: 28 April 1942, Harrow, Middlesex

- Only the second captain after Len Hutton to regain and then successfully defend the Ashes.
- The first captain to lead England to five wins in an Ashes rubber.
- Scored 312 not out on the first day for MCC Under-25s v North Zone at Peshawar in 1966/7.
- Exceeded 1,000 runs in a season 11 times, including 2,178 in 1964.
- He captained England to 18 wins in 31 Tests, including a record unbeaten 19 home Tests, and Middlesex (1971–82) to three Championship titles (plus one shared).

TEST CAREER	
BATTING	
M	39
I	66
NO	3
Runs	1,442
HSc	91
Av	22.88
100	–
50	9
Ct	52
St	–

A CULTURED, academically brilliant man, Mike Brearley was an outstanding captain. His record is unsurpassed by any other England captain.

During four years as a Cambridge Blue (two as captain) Brearley hit more runs than anyone before – 4,348 including ten centuries – and gained a first in Classics!

He went with the England side to South Africa in 1964/5 without playing in a Test match and although his appearances over the following season were limited because of his academic commitments, he led the MCC Under-25 side to Pakistan in 1966/7 and hit 312 not out on the opening day of the match against North Zone at Peshawar.

It was around this time that Brearley found himself torn between cricket and an academic life and in 1968 he took a job teaching philosophy in Newcastle, appearing for Middlesex during the summer holidays. On his own admission he was lured back to cricket by the offer of the Middlesex captaincy.

Brearley led Middlesex from 1971 to 1982, transforming the county's fortunes. During his time as captain, they won three County Championships, shared another and twice won the Gillette Cup.

Brearley's early promise as a batsman was never quite fulfilled and unquestionably he was short of Test standard. However, it has to be remembered that he was first selected as a batsman for England under Tony Greig for the first two Tests against the West Indies in 1976 and that he went with Greig's side to India in 1976/7 and made his highest score of 91 in the final Test at Bombay. He was also vice-captain to Greig and when the Sussex player's contacts with Kerry Packer were revealed, Brearley became captain of England in 1977. He insisted that Greig and the other Packer players should retain their places in the England side but also led moves to ensure that the Packer's men did not have everything their own way.

Under Brearley's captaincy, England regained the Ashes against a below-strength Australian side in 1977, but that winter while leading England in Pakistan, he broke his arm after the second Test match and could not go on the New Zealand leg of the tour.

LEP

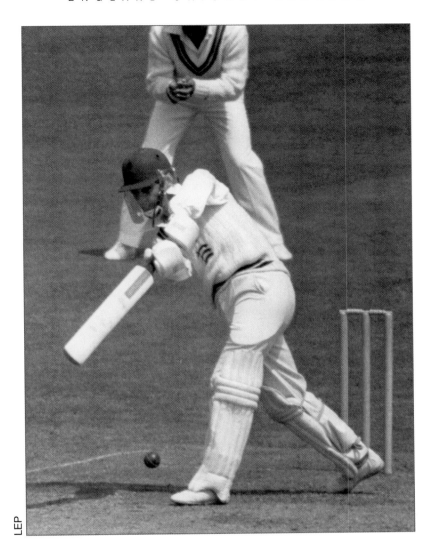

LEP

Overwhelming victories over Pakistan and New Zealand followed in 1978, and in Australia in 1978/9 England won five of the six Test matches played. Brearley was the first player to lead England to five victories in a rubber.

India were well beaten in 1979 before he took an England side 'Down Under' for a hastily arranged three-match series to help consolidate an end to the in-fighting between Kerry Packer's organisation and the Australian Board. Confronted by a full-strength Australian side, Brearley's team were beaten in all three Tests.

After the Golden Jubilee Test against India in February 1980 Brearley announced his decision to retire from Test cricket. However, after England performed miserably under Botham's captaincy against the Australians, he was persuaded to lead the team in the last four Tests. Three of them were won – two in amazing circumstances. Brearley, whose great strength was as a communicator, established a rapport with each member of his team, especially his bowlers, and both Botham and Willis performed wonders in an epic 3–1 victory.

Brearley did not play Test cricket again but in his last season with Middlesex he hit the winning runs at Worcester to lead the county to the Championship – a fitting end to a marvellous career.

He has often been described as a ruthless captain but then many great leaders had this approach and there is no doubt that Mike Brearley achieved all the success he strove for. A man of many talents, since retiring he has concentrated on psychotherapy, teaching and writing.

Chris Broad

Born: 29 September 1957, Bristol

- On the first day of the 1980 season he hit a hundred before lunch for Gloucestershire v Oxford University at The Parks.
- In 1986 he scored 1,011 runs at 45.95 in one-day matches alone.
- He established England records at Perth in 1986/7 with his innings of 162 and opening stand of 223 with Bill Athey.
- He scored three centuries for England v Australia in the 1986/7 series, the first being his maiden three-figure innings in Test cricket.
- He was voted International Cricketer of the Year in 1987 following his performances in the Ashes and one-day matches in Australia.

CHRIS BROAD played a major role in England's all-conquering tour of Australia in 1986/7. His remarkable achievement of scoring three consecutive Ashes Test hundreds puts him in the record books with Jack Hobbs, Herbert Sutcliffe and Wally Hammond.

In his late teens Broad was a fine rugby forward, representing Bristol United, England Colleges and Clifton. But this side of his sporting life was cut short by osteomyelitis, an inflammation of the bone marrow which put him out of rugby for a whole year and also for a time threatened his cricket. This was the only first of the battles he had to fight on the road to the top.

The late Gloucestershire and England all-rounder Reg Sinfield coached the young Broad for more than ten years at Colston's School and presented him with a brand new bat in morning assembly after he had scored a hundred against Prior Park College. Broad initially played league cricket with the

Author

Downend Club (where W.G. Grace learned to play more than a century ago) and then with Long Ashton. His success with Long Ashton brought him a few games with Gloucestershire's Club and Ground team and then with the 2nd XI. Before that he had played for Gloucestershire Under-19s and Gloucestershire Young Cricketers, and at the age of 19 he played at Lord's for the first time, representing the National Association of Young Cricketers against MCC Schools.

Broad made his county debut for Gloucestershire in 1979 and spent five seasons playing for the 1st XI before leaving to join Nottinghamshire. In fact, his last match for Gloucestershire was against his future county, Broad hitting 145.

His reason for leaving Gloucestershire was frustration at the fact that the Test selectors did not go west to watch potential England players and he wanted to play for England. After just a few months at Trent Bridge he was selected for four Tests against the West Indies, making his debut at Lord's where he scored a brave 55. Broad owed much to Reg Sinfield for his first cap, for it was Sinfield who wrote to the Chairman of Selectors, Peter May, and told him that the West Indies

LEP

wouldn't frighten Broad. He gave England a succession of solid starts but surprisingly was left out of the winter tour party to India. His county opening partner, Tim Robinson, was picked instead and his success coupled with Gooch's return from Test exile pushed Broad back into the shadows.

In 1986 when England tried no fewer than six different opening partners for Gooch in the series against India and New Zealand, Chris Broad did not get a look in, but during September he hit three Championship centuries and was selected for the 1986/7 tour of Australia.

His first Test hundred – 162 – came in the second Test at Perth. He and Bill Athey established an England record with an opening stand of 223. Broad followed this with 116 at Adelaide and 112 at Melbourne in the fourth Test to help regain the Ashes. Broad scored 487 runs at 69.57 and was named International Cricketer of the Year for his performances in the Tests and his prolific one-day run-getting. The tour had earned him a permanent place in the history of the game.

Occasionally his reaction to being dismissed was embarrassing: in the Lahore Test of 1987/8 he refused to leave the crease after being given out caught and in the Centenary Test at Sydney, when he was bowled for 139, he demolished his wicket. There could be something in the fact that he scored centuries during the Tests that followed these outbursts – 116 at Faislabad and 114 at Christchurch.

In 1990 Broad hit his highest first-class score, 227 not out against Kent. Two seasons later he returned to the West Country to play for Gloucestershire where sadly an arthritic hip condition forced his retirement.

Andy Caddick

Born: 21 November 1968, Christchurch, New Zealand

- He took 7 for 46 for England v South Africa at Durban in 1999/2000.
- His best bowling performance in the County Championship came against Lancashire at Taunton in 1993 when he had figures of 9 for 32.
- He was a *Wisden* Cricketer of the Year in 2000.

TEST CAREER	
BATTING	
M	53
I	81
NO	9
Runs	773
HSc	49*
Av	10.73
100	–
50	–
BOWLING	
Runs	5,769
Wkts	200
Av	28.85
Best	7-46
5w	10
10w	–
Ct	18
St	–

ANDY CADDICK, who now forms a highly successful new-ball partnership with Darren Gough, learned the game at school in Christchuch, New Zealand. He was selected as a tearaway for the Youth World Cup in Australia but decided to move to England to play club cricket for Hampstead because of a lack of encouragement and finance in his native province of Canterbury.

Two influential events occurred during Caddick's four-year qualification period. The first was that Somerset's then manager Jack Birkenshaw heard about him and enticed him to Taunton. The second was the stress fracture in his back halfway through his first season for Somerset's 2nd XI; it was cured by rest. This injury helped to convince Caddick to become a fast-medium bowler, concentrating on accuracy, bounce and the odd quick delivery, rather than a short-lived tearaway.

During the summer of 1991 Caddick took 96 2nd XI wickets for Somerset at just over 12 runs apiece but when he was called up for his first-class debut against the West Indies, he was made to pay for pitching too short. Nevertheless, his potential was unmistakable.

His qualification period served – he played for Clevedon – Caddick began the 1992 season as the county's main strike bowler, finishing the campaign with 71 wickets at 27.01, one place below Martin McCague in the national averages and rather more entitled to be considered as English!

Caddick no longer had to rely on his usefulness as a trained plasterer/tiler and odd jobman for his winter employment for in 1992/3 he was taken to Australia with the England 'A' side. The following summer in the game against Lancashire at Taunton, Caddick produced his best-ever bowling figures of 9 for 32 (12 for 120 in the match) in a sensational last innings performance.

Caddick made his England debut against Australia at Old Trafford in June 1993, claiming Allan Border as his first Test victim. He was England's leading wicket-taker on the West Indies tour of 1993/4 when he claimed 18 victims at 30.27 and had a best return of 6 for 65 in the third Test at Port-of-Spain, Trinidad. But his international career was put on hold until he returned with two 5-wicket hauls in Tests against Australia at Edgbaston in 1997 (5 for 50) and at The Oval (5 for 42) – England won both matches.

Since then Andy Caddick's Test career has blossomed. He was chosen as Whyte & Mackay's Bowler of the Year in 1997 and the following season became the country's leading wicket-taker with 105 first-class victims. Twenty wickets at 20.60 in the four-match series against New Zealand in 1999 confirmed his growing stature in the game. The following winter he toured South Africa and in the third Test at Kingsmead, Durban, he produced his best-ever figures for England, taking 7 for 46 as the home side were bowled out for 156.

He added another 22 Test wickets at less than 20 runs apiece in the 2000 series against the West Indies and also became only the fourth England bowler to take four wickets in an over when he routed the tourists in a 5 for 14 burst at Headingley. Though he returned from Pakistan and Sri Lanka with a

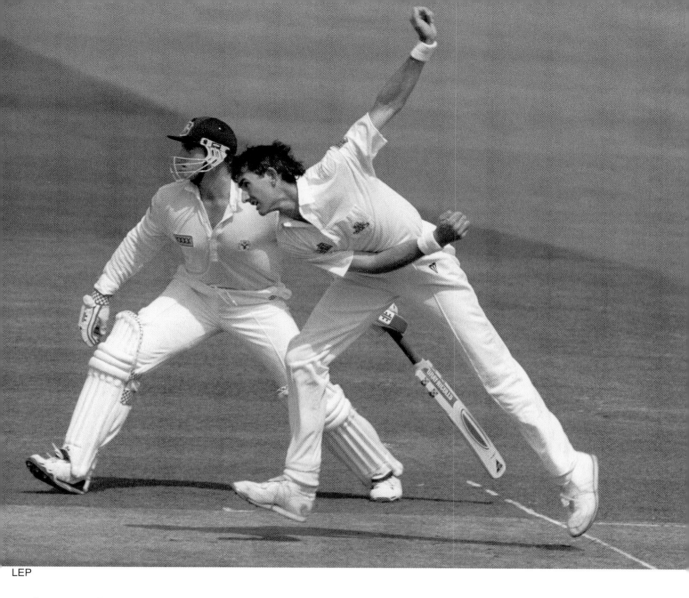

modest reward on unresponsive pitches, he fully deserved the new contract he received for the Ashes series of 2001. Along with Glamorgan's Robert Croft, he refused to tour India following the atrocities of 11 September 2001 but was reinstated for the tour of his native New Zealand. There he not only topped the bowling averages with 19 wickets at 19.84 runs apiece but also became only the ninth English bowler to reach 200 Test wickets.

Brian Close

Born: 24 February 1931, Rawdon, Leeds

- At 18 years 149 days, he remains the youngest player to represent England.
- He did the double in 1949 and 1952, the youngest man to achieve this feat and the only player to do so in his first season.
- He exceeded 1,000 runs in a season 20 times and 100 wickets twice.
- His career tally of 813 catches is the fifth highest in first-class cricket.

TEST CAREER

BATTING

M	22
I	37
NO	2
Runs	887
HSc	70
Av	25.34
100	–
50	4

BOWLING

Runs	532
Wkts	18
Av	29.55
Best	4-35
5w	–
10w	–
Ct	24
St	–

CRICKETERS do not come any more determined or courageous than Brian Close, a hard-hitting left-handed batsman, off-break or seam right-arm bowler and one of the greatest close-to-the-wicket fielders in the history of the game. He captained Yorkshire from 1963 to 1970 and led them to four Championship titles.

So much was expected of Close in the light of his deeds as a boy that he missed the acclamations which a normal player of his calibre would stimulate – certainly Yorkshire supporters and many beyond the stone grey walls that twist and turn through the great cricketing county believe that England could have used his talents a good deal more than they did.

In 1949, his first season of first-class cricket, Close did the double aged 18 – a phenomenal record for a youngster – and made his Test debut against New Zealand at Old Trafford. In fact, Close is still the youngest player to represent England in a Test match. Sadly he was out for a duck and took 1 for 85. In the winter of 1950/1 he was on the boat to Australia as a member of Freddie Brown's party which secured an elusive victory in the last of the five-match series. He made 108 in the opening first-class match but in the only Test he played, he was out for 0 and 1 – there were many who thought he had been pitched in at the deep end of Test cricket too soon. Certainly these early failures may well have influenced his subsequent Test career which ran intermittently.

In 1961 considerable blame was heaped upon his broad shoulders for getting out to a rash shot in a Test match against Australia – he didn't play again for England for two years. Yet when facing Hall, Griffith, Sobers and Gibbs of the strong West Indies side he established himself at last, playing an heroic innings of 70 at Lord's, during which he drove Wes Hall to distraction by moving down the pitch towards him as he ran up to bowl.

Something of a cricket eccentric, honest and caring to other players, he was a most popular choice to lead England after they had been overwhelmed by the West Indies for much of the 1966 series. Under Close's leadership, England won the last Test at The Oval by an innings and 34 runs. He seemed to symbolise all that the supporters looked for. He was a no-nonsense professional and an astute tactician. Close was unquestionably a national hero, but sadly his reign was to be short lived.

In 1967 he led England to victory over India and Pakistan and he was invited to captain the side to the Caribbean. Late in the season he used delaying tactics in a vital County Championship match against Warwickshire, slowing down the over-rate at the end of the match to prevent Warwickshire from winning. He had a brush with a spectator and MCC withdrew their invitation to lead the side to the West Indies.

Close left Yorkshire after a disagreement regarding his attitude to one-day cricket and took over at Somerset, whose status he helped raise, particularly in one-day cricket! At Tony Greig's insistence, Close was recalled to the England side for three Tests against the West Indies in 1976 when he was 45 years old, batting and fielding as bravely as ever. He retired from county cricket at the end of the following

LEP

season but he appeared in the Scarborough Festival until he was 55. Since then he has been an England selector and manager and Chairman of Yorkshire.

Denis Compton

Born: 23 May 1918, Hendon, Middlesex
Died: 23 April 1997

- He scored 102 in his first Test v Australia and at 20 years 19 days remains England's youngest century maker.
- His 278 in 290 minutes remains the highest Test score at Trent Bridge and the record in England v Pakistan Tests.
- He scored 1,004 runs in his debut season, the youngest to achieve this feat.
- He exceeded 1,000 runs in a season 14 times (plus 3 overseas), including 2,000 on six occasions.
- His 3,816 runs and 18 hundreds in 1947 remain world records for any season.
- He scored 300 not out in 181 minutes for MCC v North Eastern Transvaal at Benoni in 1948/9 – still the fastest 300 in all first-class cricket.
- In all first-class matches at Lord's he scored 16,732 runs (average 48.08) and 48 hundreds.

TEST CAREER

BATTING

M	78
I	131
NO	15
Runs	5,807
HSc	278
Av	50.06
100	17
50	28

BOWLING

Runs	1,410
Wkts	25
Av	56.40
Best	5-70
5w	1
10w	–
Ct	49
St	–

DENIS COMPTON was a popular and colourful sporting hero in the Britain of the 1940s. A natural at both cricket and football, he thrilled the crowds with his unorthodox and at times cheeky play.

Few English batsmen have risen to the top at an earlier age than Compton. At just 18 in 1936 he played his first match for Middlesex against Sussex, batting number 11 in the Whitsun match at Lord's. Within a month he had made the first of his 123 first-class centuries and by the end of the season there were many who thought he should have gone to Australia with Gubby Allen's MCC side. He played in his first Test against New Zealand in the following year and in all the subsequent home Tests up to the outbreak of war, making 102 in his first innings against Australia at Trent Bridge in 1938.

Towards the end of the hostilities he played some first-class cricket in India and returned in excellent form for the 1946 season. In Australia that winter he made a hundred in each innings of the Adelaide Test. Back in England in 1947 he embarked on his golden year and his memorable record-breaking partnerships with Bill Edrich.

When he had made a hundred, he often considered that enough, unless the requirements of the side made it important for him to go on. In 1947, with Middlesex challenging successfully for the County Championship, he went on often! His 1947 record of 3,816 runs and 18 centuries in a season is unlikely ever to be beaten, especially now that the amount of first-class cricket being played in England is decreasing.

However, in the last match of 1947 his knee let him down and he was seldom free of pain or discomfort afterwards. Yet in 1948 he played what many regard as his greatest innings – an unbeaten 145 against Australia at Old Trafford, overcoming Ray Lindwall at his most hostile and after being knocked out and retiring hurt early in his innings. He went to South Africa in 1948/9 and made his famous 300 in three hours at Benoni, easily the fastest triple century ever made. Though in the following season he reached the peak of his football career, he missed most of that summer as the result of an operation to remove a fragment of bone from his right knee. Characteristically he returned with a century against Surrey in August, but the knee continued to trouble him.

In 1954 he was still able to play an astonishing innings of 278 in a little under a run a minute against Pakistan at Trent Bridge, but in November 1955 he had to have his kneecap removed. Again he returned with a hundred – against Somerset – and when fit enough to play in the last Test against Australia in 1956, he made a brilliant 94.

ES

Compton captained Middlesex jointly with Bill Edrich in 1951 and 1952, an unusual arrangement which recognised the talents of two outstanding players, but he had perhaps too much of the cavalier spirit to be an outstanding captain.

After the 1957 season he retired, making 143 and 48 in his last match for Middlesex. For a while he was a commentator on Test matches for BBC television.

As a footballer, Compton played as a dashing left-winger for Arsenal from 1936 to 1950. He won a League Championship medal in 1948 and in his second-last match, an FA Cup Winners medal. These were his only football honours because the war took his best years and although he was a wartime international for England, he did not make the official list.

Dominic Cork

Born: 7 August 1971, Newcastle-under-Lyme, Staffordshire

- *Wisden* Cricketer of the Year in 1995.
- He performed the hat trick v West Indies at Old Trafford in 1995 – the first in Test history to occur in the opening over of a day's play.
- His best bowling figures at Test level are 7 for 43 v West Indies at Lord's in 1995.
- He took 8 for 53 for Derbyshire v Essex at Derby before lunch on his 20th birthday.
- His best bowling figures in the County Championship are 9 for 43 for Derbyshire v Northamptonshire at Derby in 1995.

TEST CAREER

BATTING

M	34
I	53
NO	8
Runs	781
HSc	59
Av	17.35
100	–
50	2

BOWLING

Runs	3,647
Wkts	124
Av	29.41
Best	7-43
5w	5
10w	–
Ct	17
St	–

SINCE TAKING a wicket in his very first over for Derbyshire against New Zealand in 1990, Dominic Cork has hogged the headlines during a controversial career. That summer he played for Young England against Pakistan and after match figures of 8 for 91 in the victory at Headingley, he preserved the series when he came in as nightwatchman in the third 'Test' at Taunton with the home side facing an innings defeat and steered them towards safety with a battling 110.

He went to New Zealand in 1990/1, sharing lodgings with Yorkshire's Darren Gough and playing for East Shirley in Christchurch. He returned with a back problem but fortunately it was not as severe as he had feared. He saw two specialists in New Zealand, both of whom diagnosed a stress fracture, but on his return to Derby he immediately saw another specialist who said that the stiffness resulted from the fact that he was still growing. The county were aware of this and were keen to allow him to develop at his own pace.

In June 1991 he found his way back into the 1st XI. Immediately he began to take wickets, threes and fours, making up 30 in the games before he encountered Essex at Derby in August. A muggy, overcast morning favoured seam and swing bowling and on his twentieth birthday Cork made such inroads into the Essex batting that he took 8 for 53 before lunch. Not since Bill Copson took 8 for 11 against Warwickshire in 1937 had a Derbyshire bowler enjoyed such a prosperous session. It was an outstandingly mature performance which gave Derbyshire their first Championship win over Essex for twenty-five years.

Cork is blessed with a classically high action, a lively pace which allows him to bowl an awkward bouncer and an ability to bowl a stock ball which is delivered from close to the stumps and leaves the right-hander from middle and off. Yet when he returned from the England 'A' tour to West Indies in 1991/2 he was nipping the ball in during a successful Benson & Hedges spell against Durham at Jesmond. There were suggestions that the England team manager Keith Fletcher had tried to make Cork bowl faster in the Caribbean and Derbyshire coach Phil Russell wrote a letter outlining the county's case that Cork was more effective as a medium-pace swing bowler. It became public knowledge and there were some who tried to build this into another Derbyshire v the Establishment row.

After making four England 'A' tours, he was finally rewarded with a Test debut against the West Indies at Lord's in 1995: he celebrated with figures of 7 for 43. He went on to take a hat trick in the fourth Test of that series at Old Trafford – the first by an Englishman in thirty years. Not surprisingly his performances in the summer of 1995 were recognised by *Wisden* which made him one of its five 'Cricketers of the Year'. But just when a glittering Test future appeared to beckon, he missed England's 1996/7 winter tour for personal reasons, joining the team briefly on the New Zealand leg. He returned to thrilling form against the West Indies in the summer of 2000, playing a crucial defiant innings to steer England to victory at Lord's. He missed England's winter tours to Pakistan and Sri Lanka but then returned to the fold for 2001's Ashes series.

Dominic Cork is a ferocious competitor with an appetite for defying those who wrote him off at international level.

Colin Cowdrey

Born: 24 December 1932, Putumala, Ootacamund, India
Died: 4 December 2000, Angmering, Sussex

TEST CAREER	
BATTING	
M	114
I	188
NO	15
Runs	7,624
HSc	182
Av	44.06
100	22
50	38
BOWLING	
Runs	104
Wkts	0
Av	–
Best	–
5w	–
10w	–
Ct	120
St	–

- He shared with Peter May in a stand of 411 v West Indies at Edgbaston in 1957. It remains England's highest score for any wicket.
- He set a Test record by winning nine successive tosses.
- He became the second non-wicket-keeper after Wally Hammond to hold 100 catches in Test matches.
- He was the first player to appear in 100 Test matches.
- He scored 307 for MCC v South Australia at Adelaide in 1962/3 – the highest score by any touring batsman in Australia.
- He ended his Test career with then world records of 114 matches, 7,624 runs, 22 hundreds and 120 catches.
- He was the youngest player to be capped by Kent.
- He was the 16th batsman to score 100 first-class hundreds.
- He exceeded 1,000 runs 27 times (including six occasions overseas), a feat bettered only by W.G. Grace and Frank Woolley with 28 each.

FEW PLAYERS in the world have spent longer at the top in post-war cricket than Colin Cowdrey, whose Test career began in Australia in 1954/5. When he retired, his 114 Tests were a record and his 7,624 Test runs were the record for an Englishman.

Cowdrey first played for Kent in 1950. The following year he made an impressive 106 for the Gentlemen against a strong Players side at Scarborough. Two half-centuries for the Gentlemen against

the Australians at Lord's in 1953 confirmed his swift advance towards the England team. In 1954, when he was captain of Oxford University, he was 12th man in the last Test against Pakistan at The Oval and was a somewhat unexpected selection for the MCC tour of Australia and New Zealand.

The tour began tragically for him: on arrival in Perth he learned of the sudden death of his father, who had been a tremendous inspiration to his cricket. However, it was Cowdrey's stand with Peter May that turned the second Test and the series in England's favour. His remarkable innings of 102 – out of his side's total of only 191 – started England on the way to success in the third Test.

In his early days in the Test side England were strong in bowling but not in late-order batting and the innings would thrive or fall with Cowdrey and May. It was their historic stand of 411 at Edgbaston in the summer of 1957 that had a decisive effect on the series with West Indies. Cowdrey followed 150 at Edgbaston with 152 in the next Test at Lord's. As an opening batsman in the West Indies in 1960 Cowdrey met the pace bowlers with courage and success and when Peter May was taken ill, he assumed the captaincy that he had first taken over from May in 1959.

In Australia in 1962/3 Cowdrey made his highest first-class score, 307 against South Australia in Adelaide. Later in 1963 in the Lord's Test against West Indies, his arm was broken by a short ball from Wes Hall. At the end of a dramatic match he had to come in for the last two balls to earn England a draw – which he did, fortunately as the non-striker.

In 1966 Cowdrey became captain again in place of M.J.K. Smith but after England had been beaten at Headingley he was replaced by Brian Close. He took over again when Close, having recently been censured for unfair play, proved unacceptable to the MCC Committee selecting for the tour of the West Indies in 1967/8. He batted magnificently on that tour, scoring 534 runs in the Test series, including 71 at Port-of-Spain to clinch the rubber. The following summer saw Cowdrey play in his hundredth Test match against the Australians at Edgbaston. To celebrate this achievement, he hit yet another Test century.

One morning in December 1974 Colin Cowdrey's usual routine was shattered by a phone call from Mike Denness in Australia. Injuries had ravaged the touring party and Colin, aged 42, was needed to join the rest of the team in their battle against Lillee and Thomson. He responded with skill and character and managed to score his last century against the Australians – his innings of 151 not out steering Kent to victory by four wickets.

In 1986 Colin Cowdrey's appointment as MCC President for the county's bicentenary in 1987 was well received by all connected with Kent cricket. Later he became chairman of the International Cricket Council. He was knighted in 1992 and raised to the peerage five years later. Lord Cowdrey of Tonbridge was a true sportsman, charming, gentle and friendly. He was true to himself and to the game he loved – the ideal and happy cricketer for Kent and England.

LEP

Mike Denness

Born: 1 December 1940, Bellshill, Lanarkshire, Scotland

- His highest score in Test cricket – 188 – is the highest by an England captain in Australia.
- He exceeded 1,000 runs in a season 14 times (plus once on tour).

MIKE DENNESS was a naturally aggressive opening or early middle-order batsman, an elegant stroke-maker with an array of attractive shots.

He was an outstanding schoolboy player at Ayr Academy where he was coached by former Sussex player, Charlie Oakes. In 1959 he became the first schoolboy to be capped by Scotland. Also playing in Scotland games was the former Kent all-rounder Jim Allan and it was on his recommendation that Les Ames invited Denness to Canterbury for a month's trial in 1961.

The following year saw him join Kent on a special registration, appearing for the first time in July against Essex. Unfortunately he had to face Jim Laker on a turning wicket and failed to trouble the scorers. In 1963 Denness topped 1,000 runs in a season for the first time and continued to do so every season for much of his first-class career.

When Kent won the County Championship in 1970, their centenary year, Mike Denness stepped in efficiently to lead the side when Colin Cowdrey was on Test match duty. It didn't affect his batting: he scored 1,494 runs at 40.37. Against Essex Denness scored 167 on the opening day, leading Kent to a fine win. He followed this with victory over Hampshire at Maidstone and then, when Cowdrey returned, he hit another hundred in the defeat of Somerset.

Denness had played only once for England, against New Zealand at The Oval in 1969, before being appointed vice-captain to Tony Lewis for the tour to India in 1972/3. He played skilfully against the Indian spinners and it was apparent that he was the most likely candidate to succeed Ray Illingworth. Denness did not play against West Indies or New Zealand in 1973 but he led the side to the Caribbean the following winter and England drew the series. England won all three Tests against India in 1974 and Denness hit two centuries – 118 at Lord's and 100 at Edgbaston.

His downfall came in Australia in the 1974/5 series. England were in disarray against the pace and fire of Lillee and Thomson, and Denness dropped himself from the fourth Test match at Sydney after a run of poor scores. He returned for the next match and in the sixth, with Thomson absent, he hit 188. He followed this with an innings of 181 in New Zealand and he led England to the semi-final of the World Cup. Confronted again by the pace of Lillee and Thomson, England lost by an innings in the first Test of the series against Australia that followed the World Cup in the summer of 1975. Denness was dropped from the next and did not appear again in Test cricket.

An outwardly tough but inwardly sensitive Scotsman with no flair for handling the demands of the press and not a natural 'man-manager', he nevertheless captained Kent with outstanding success, notably in one-day cricket. He was a generally sound, orthodox and enthusiastic captain on the field who set a shining example with his athletic fielding in the covers. Under his captaincy Kent won the John Player League three times, the Benson & Hedges Cup twice and the Gillette Cup once but in 1976 he was relieved of the captaincy as politics raged within the county.

In 1977 he moved to Essex and played a significant role in helping the county win their first-ever Championship in 1979. Denness, who was an outstanding fly-half and would certainly have gained a Scotland rugby cap, later worked in insurance, finance and as a manager for World Series cricket teams.

Author

Ted Dexter

Born: 15 May 1935, Milan, Italy

- His highest Test score of 205 is England's only double century in Pakistan.
- He completed a record aggregate of 481 by an England captain against Australia.
- He was the third English batsman after Colin Cowdrey and Ken Barrington to score 100s v all current Test playing countries.
- He exceeded 1,000 runs in a season eight times (plus twice on tour) including 2,000 on three occasions.

TEST CAREER	
BATTING	
M	62
I	102
NO	8
Runs	4,502
HSc	205
Av	47.89
100	9
50	27
BOWLING	
Runs	2,306
Wkts	66
Av	34.93
Best	4-10
5w	–
10w	–
Ct	29
St	–

KNOWN THROUGHOUT the cricketing world as 'Lord Ted', Ted Dexter was one of the most dashing batsmen and most gifted all-round cricketers to play for England in modern times.

From his early days at Radley College and Cambridge he was also a fine golfer, a tremendous hitter of the ball for whom great things were forecast. These predictions were strengthened in 1969 when, after his retirement from first-class cricket, he was runner-up in the Oxford and Cambridge Golfing Society's President's Putter.

Dexter captained Cambridge's cricket team in 1958 and two years later took over the captaincy of Sussex. He had matured early and at 25 was already established in the front rank of English cricketers. Having played his first Test against the New Zealand tourists in 1958, Dexter was sent out to Australia during the 1958/9 MCC tour when Willie Watson and Raman Subba Row were injured. He played in two Tests there and on the New Zealand section of the tour made his maiden Test century, scoring 141

in the final Test at Christchurch. A year later, after a modest home season, he was selected for the tour of the West Indies. It was a much criticised choice, but he proved to be one of the successes of the tour, playing the fast bowling with great zest and topping the Test batting averages.

His competitive temperament meant he relished the confrontation with physical danger presented by the pace of the West Indies attack and he never flinched. He was batting at number 3 when he made his second century of the series at Georgetown. There, in company with Raman Subba Row, he ensured that England could not lose the match. It was this series that above all established Ted Dexter, whose class was never in doubt, as capable of big Test innings.

In the first Test of the 1961 series against Australia he earned England a draw with a second innings of 180 and in the decisive Test of the series at Old Trafford he played a spectacular innings of 76 at a run a minute, putting England in the position of needing only 106 runs from their last nine wickets. But after Dexter's dismissal, they collapsed!

Dexter became captain of England when he took the MCC side to India and Pakistan in 1961/2. In

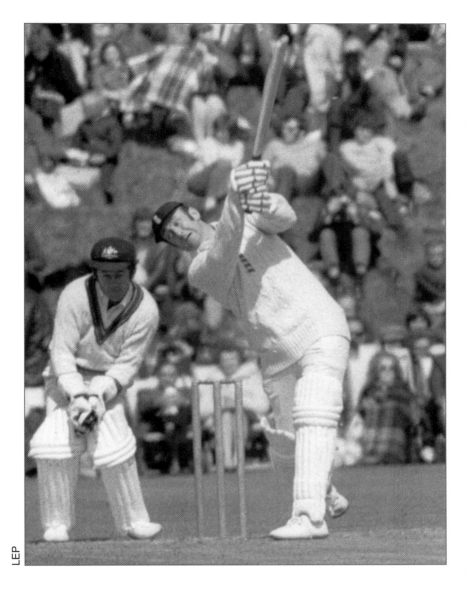

LEP

the home series against Pakistan the following summer he was captain in the first two Tests but Colin Cowdrey was preferred for the captaincy in the third. However, with Cowdrey unfit, Dexter was appointed captain for the fourth Test and subsequently led England in Australia and New Zealand in 1962/3.

Few who witnessed it will ever forget his innings of 93 in the second Test at Melbourne when he set England on the road to victory, having scored 70 and 99 in the first Test. Though he scored a number of centuries, he is best remembered by many for his innings of 70 in 81 minutes in the Lord's Test of 1963 against the West Indian fast bowlers Wes Hall and Charlie Griffith, then in their menacing prime.

He remained captain until he stood for Parliament in October 1964 and had to delay his acceptance of the invitation to tour South Africa. When he eventually went, it was as vice-captain to Mike Smith. He did not captain England again and slipped out of regular first-class cricket.

When his county's batting was depleted by injury in 1968, Dexter returned to play for Sussex and made an immediate impact, scoring 203 against Kent at Hastings in his first innings. He was then selected for the last two Tests against the Australians, the excitement his return caused further illustrating the great loss English cricket suffered when 'Lord Ted' retired. He took up numerous business interests until in 1989 he became the first paid Chairman of Selectors for England.

Graham Dilley

Born: 18 May 1959, Dartford, Kent

- He performed two hat tricks – once for Kent v Surrey at The Oval in 1985 and once v Essex at Chelmsford in 1986.

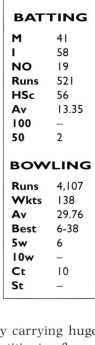
GRAHAM DILLEYwas only 21 when Clive Lloyd called him the fastest white bowler in the world. If he had been blessed with a stronger skeletal system and the support of another genuinely quick bowler throughout the 1980s, England would probably have enjoyed a great deal more Test success.

The circumstances of Dilley's rise from a promising fast bowler to the leader of England's attack were unusual to say the least. He learned his cricket playing with his father and brother on Dartford Heath and after progressing through various school teams he was given the opportunity of Saturday morning net practice with Kent. However, when he left school he had to take a job as a diamond setter in Hatton Garden. He soon gave this job up when he was offered the chance to play for the Kent 2nd XI in midweek games. During the winter months he would build up

his strength for the coming summer by carrying huge sheets of plasterboard for his uncle's partitioning firm.

Dilley first played for Kent in 1977 but did not make his Championship debut until the following year, taking 5 for 32 against Middlesex at Lord's. During the course of that summer he gained early international honours playing for England against the West Indies in the Agatha Christie Under-19 Test series. His early performances had been enough to convince Mike Brearley and the Test selectors that he was a worthy choice to tour Australia in the winter of 1979/80. So, despite still being uncapped by Kent, he packed his bags for 'Down Under'. He was selected to tour on the basis that he was going to gain experience but he was chosen for the first Test ahead of players like Bob Willis, who was struggling for form and fitness. At Perth he added his name to the scorecard with: Lillee, caught Willey, bowled Dilley.

The following summer he represented England in three rain-interrupted Test matches against the West Indies, taking 11 wickets at 16.63 runs apiece. In 1980/1 Dilley toured the Caribbean and though he only took ten wickets at a rather expensive average, he bowled fast enough to impress such discerning judges as Lloyd. In Botham's 1981 Ashes triumph he took 16 wickets at 19.64 runs apiece. His best – 4 for 24 at Trent Bridge – came in the only match Australia won!

In 1984 Dilley and his doctors feared his career was finished because of back trouble and from February 1984 to June 1986 he played no Test cricket. But he worked hard on his strength and fitness and out of the turmoil came a renewed paceman. He performed the hat trick for Kent against Surrey at

LEP

LEP

The Oval in 1985 and against Essex at Chelmsford in 1986. Sandwiched in between was a season with Natal in South Africa, refining his delivery and his change of pace.

He reached peak form in Australia in 1986/7 when, controlling his length and off-stump line superbly, he moved his staple outswinger lethally late – his 5 for 68 at Brisbane helping England retain the Ashes. Dilley's great determination was reflected when Pakistan made 708 at The Oval in 1987, his 6 for 154 an indication of his refusal to give in.

At the end of the 1986 season Kent revealed that Dilley had refused to sign a new two-year contract but it also came to light that he had asked to be released some twelve months earlier. On becoming a free agent under TCCB rules, he joined Worcestershire, whom he helped to the County Championship and Sunday League crown in 1988. He spent six seasons at New Road, many of them plagued by knee and ankle problems, but his enforced retirement in 1992 was brought about by a recurrence of the neck injury that cut short his tour of Pakistan in 1984.

Basil D'Oliveira

Born: 4 October 1931, Signal Hill, Cape Town, South Africa

- He exceeded 1,000 runs in a season nine times.
- In the second Test against Pakistan at Dacca in 1968/9 he scored 114 not out from a total of 174 on a pitch totally pitted with holes.

TEST CAREER	
BATTING	
M	44
I	70
NO	8
Runs	2,484
HSc	158
Av	40.06
100	5
50	15
BOWLING	
Runs	1,859
Wkts	47
Av	39.55
Best	3-46
5w	–
10w	–
Ct	29
St	–

BASIL D'OLIVEIRA became more significant than he could possibly have imagined when he walked on to the field to play for England at Lord's in 1966. He gave new and hitherto unimagined hope to millions of black South Africans.

As early as 1956 D'Oliveira had begun to write from his Cape Town home to England in the hope of finding coaching instruction so that he could help to teach the game to others in his community.

He performed with such dazzling success in minor cricket on very poor grounds and matting wickets that word of his talent reached England via John Arlott and Glamorgan's Peter Walker. As a result he was invited to join Middleton in the Central Lancashire League on a fairly poorly paid contract. He needed £200 for the air fare and the sum was partially raised by raffles, fêtes and matches held in the area around his tenement home, but for 'Dolly', as he became known, it was a wise investment. It took him some time to adapt to English conditions but by the end of the 1960 season he was ahead of Gary Sobers at the top of the league batting averages!

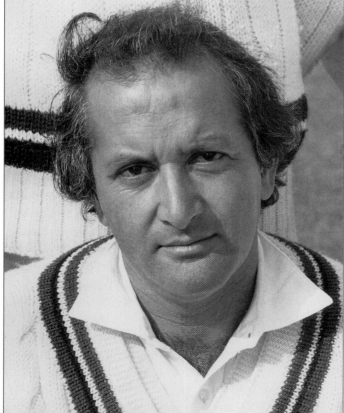

He played with great success for Middleton for four years, made his first-class debut in Rhodesia in a Commonwealth XI tour in 1961/2 and on a later Commonwealth tour Tom Graveney persuaded him that he could make the grade in county cricket. He spent 1964 qualifying for Worcestershire, making a century against the Australians, and in 1965 at the age of 33 he was the only batsman in the County Championship to score more than 1,500 runs.

D'Oliveira found it difficult to believe that he had been picked to play for England against the West Indies at Lord's in 1966. It is said that he was so proud of his England cap that he wore it in bed.

'Dolly' was a natural player – a most effective batsman with a sound defence and immensely strong forearms who hit the ball with astonishing power and perfect timing. He used his feet well, drove fiercely off the back foot and was a magnificent puller and cutter. His right-arm medium-pace swing bowling with its classic action proved a frequent breaker of awkward partnerships.

LEP

D'Oliveira was more or less a regular in the England side for six years, making his highest score of 158 in the final Test against Australia at The Oval in 1968 as he and Derek Underwood (7 for 50) effectively won the Test.

Later that year he was the innocent cause of an international incident when, picked to replace Tom Cartwright for the MCC tour of South Africa after he had been controversially omitted in the first place, he was refused entry and the tour was cancelled.

Long after losing his place in the England side to Tony Greig, D'Oliveira continued to display his class for Worcestershire. He was capable of anything when the mood was right, once almost winning a Benson & Hedges Cup Final at Lord's single-handed despite a severe leg injury, and keeping Yorkshire in the field for more than a day while compiling 227 at Hull in 1974 – purely because a Yorkshire bowler had annoyed him with a reference to his colour!

On retiring in 1979 he became Worcestershire's coach, enjoying watching his son Damian play for the county. A man of rare, fighting qualities, he overcame many hurdles in his unprecedented career, doing honour to the game of cricket and to his people.

Bill Edrich

Born: 26 March 1916, Lingwood, Norfolk
Died: 24 April 1986, Whitehall Court, Chesham, Buckinghamshire

- He exceeded 1,000 runs in a season 15 times, including 2000 on nine occasions and 3,539 (an aggregate only exceeded by Denis Compton) in 1947.
- He scored nine double centuries, including eight for Middlesex.
- He carried his bat for 140 not out of 303 for Lord Tennyson's XI v Sind at Karachi in 1937/8 on his debut in India.
- He had scored 1,010 runs before June 1938, the fifth Englishman after W.G. Grace, Tom Hayward, Wally Hammond and Charlie Hallows to achieve this feat.
- He shared an unbeaten stand of 424 with Denis Compton for Middlesex v Somerset at Lord's in 1948. This remains the third-wicket record in English first-class cricket and the highest for any wicket at Lord's.

TEST CAREER

BATTING

M	39
I	63
NO	2
Runs	2,440
HSc	219
Av	40.00
100	6
50	13

BOWLING

Runs	1,693
Wkts	41
Av	41.29
Best	4-68
5w	–
10w	–
Ct	39
St	–

BILL EDRICH (on the left in the picture) made his debut as a young cricketer for Norfolk in the Minor Counties Championship of 1934. Thirty-five years later in 1969 he was back playing for them. During the intervening decades Edrich had gained fame as one half of a partnership that had devastated bowling for both Middlesex and England immediately after the Second World War – Compton was the other half.

Edrich was also a good footballer and played a number of games for Tottenham Hotspur, but it was as a professional cricketer that he established himself at an early age. Qualifying for Middlesex in 1937, he came on the county scene as Patsy Hendren was in his last season and Denis Compton was just starting out. Though lacking the genius or the range of Compton, Edrich had other qualities – courage, fearlessness, resolution in adversity – that imprinted themselves on the imagination of the cricketing public.

In only his second full season for Middlesex he joined the select band of batsmen who have made 1,000 runs before the end of May and he played in four Tests against Don Bradman's 1938 Australians. But he met with little success and during both that series and the subsequent tour of South Africa the selectors were often criticised for their persistence in picking him. However, in the last Test in South Africa – the notorious 'timeless' Test in Durban – he made a magnificent 219 in the second innings. After the war the selectors' faith was handsomely justified.

Edrich returned to Middlesex after distinguished service in the RAF. He won the DFC as a bomber pilot.

He played only once against India in 1946 but was one of the great successes of the 1946/7 tour of Australia where his courageous displays against the fast bowlers left him bruised but not bewildered. Then he turned amateur.

His partnerships with Denis Compton in 1947 for Middlesex in their Championship-winning year and for England against South Africa are legendary. Among the most remarkable were an unbroken stand of 287 in just over two-and-a-half hours against Surrey at The Oval, another stand of 227 in a little over two hours at Leicester and 370 in the Lord's Test. At Grace Road they opened the second innings with 66 runs needed in 25 minutes and made them with seven minutes to spare. In that season Bill Edrich made 3,539 runs, an aggregate exceeded in cricket history only by Denis Compton – in the same year.

Unfortunately Edrich did not often approach his golden form in later seasons and was not chosen to go to Australia in 1950/1. But four years later, with England short of opening batsmen, he was picked as a tough warrior who would not be overcome by the big occasion.

ES

Sturdily built, he was short of inches and yet he seemed to relish facing a fast bowler. A brave hooker and a quick cutter, he was particularly adept at the pulled drive. It was not a classic or attractive method but allied to his pugnacious temperament it was good to watch and effective.

In his heyday Edrich had been a fast bowler who from just a few yards run and with a slinging action worked up surprising pace and took some useful wickets. In later years he acquired a happy touch as joint-captain of Middlesex with Compton for two seasons and as captain from 1953 to 1957.

Married five times, he was certainly a man who lived life to the full and played his cricket the same way.

John Edrich

Born: 21 June 1937, Blofield, Norfolk

- His score of 310 not out v New Zealand at Headingley in 1965 is the highest score for England by a left-hander – it included five sixes and 52 fours, the most boundaries in any Test.
- He exceeded 1,000 runs in a season 19 times (plus twice overseas), including 2,000 on six occasions.
- He scored nine successive fifties in 1965, the most in England since 1926.
- He became the third left-hander after Philip Mead and Frank Woolley to score 100 hundreds when he made 101 not out for Surrey v Derbyshire at The Oval in 1977.
- He scored the first fifty and won the first match award in a limited-overs international against Australia at Melbourne in 1970/1.

TEST CAREER

BATTING

M	77
I	127
NO	9
Runs	5,138
HSc	310*
Av	43.54
100	12
50	24

BOWLING

Runs	23
Wkts	0
Av	–
Best	1-20
5w	–
10w	–
Ct	43
St	–

TENACIOUS, courageous and totally phlegmatic, John Edrich served England loyally over 13 years and 77 Tests.

A cousin of the former England and Middlesex batsman Bill Edrich, John left Norfolk some twenty years after his famed relation but rather than go to Middlesex, he opted for Surrey. In 1959, his first full season, he had made 1,799 runs including a century in each innings of his second Championship match, during which he was struck on the left hand by a lively ball from Fred Trueman. The injury healed only slowly and was again badly damaged by Tyson in the last match of the season. An orthopaedic surgeon finally solved the problem by grafting a piece of leg bone

into the hand, giving rise to the story that Edrich was the only batsman who could be struck on the hand and given out lbw!

It was 1963 before he played in his first Test against West Indies. He went to India with M.J.K. Smith's MCC team that winter but was one of many taken ill there and it was not until his innings of 120 against Australia in the second Test at Lord's in 1964 that he established himself as a Test batsman.

The following summer he enjoyed some astonishing success. From early June 1965 he played successive innings of 139 against the New Zealanders; 121 not out v Oxford University; 205 not out v Gloucestershire; 55 v Kent; 96 v Essex; 188 v Northamptonshire; 92 and 105 v Yorkshire on a bad wicket at Bradford; and 310 not out in the Headingley Test against New Zealand. But then the run ended. In the first Test against South Africa at Lord's, he was hit on the head by a ball bowled by Peter Pollock and it was some time before he was fully fit again. The valuable innings he played in Australia that winter, 109 in the second Test, 103 in the third and 85 in the fifth – all at number 3 – were compiled in the more patient, controlled method which he deployed remarkably consistently thereafter.

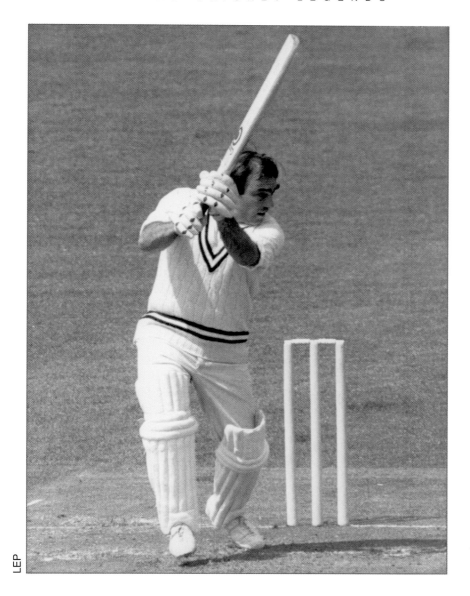

LEP

In 1969 when England lost the bulk of its experienced batting – Ken Barrington, Colin Cowdrey and Tom Graveney – there was still Edrich. He illustrated his pre-eminence by finishing the season far ahead of the field on top of the first-class batting averages, having made 2,238 runs at an average of 69.93.

After a fine tour of Australia in 1970/1 he lost some consistency and his Test place. His future seemed to lie in a new role as Surrey's captain, but England could not manage without his resolution and he returned in 1974/5 when the Australian pace attack broke hearts as well as fingers. At Sydney Edrich had two ribs cracked by a short ball from Lillee. Giving not an inch of ground, the 38-year-old then had an outstanding home series on slower pitches against the same tormentors. He piled up 175 at Lord's – his seventh century against the Australians – and at The Oval he was bowled by Lillee four runs short of yet another century. A year later he was called up again and batted resolutely against the fierce West Indies pace attack.

In the relative tranquillity of county cricket, Edrich, who scored 29,305 first-class runs for Surrey at an average of 46.07, became the 18th batsman to score 100 centuries when he made 101 not out against Derbyshire at The Oval. Later the same month he scored two centuries in the match against Kent. In 1977 he was made an MBE and he retired a year later.

John Emburey

Born: 20 August 1952, Peckham, London

- He dismissed New Zealand's opening batsman, Bruce Edgar, with his fourth ball in Test cricket.
- His analysis of 6 for 33, which included a spell of 5 for 5, remains the record for any visiting bowler in a Test in Sri Lanka.
- In 1983 he won the Swanton Trophy for being the first bowler to reach the 100 wicket mark.
- He hit six sixes off seven balls for Western Province v Eastern Province at Cape Town in 1983/4.
- He established a world first-class record by scoring 46 entirely in boundaries (a six and ten fours) for England XI v Tasmania at Hobart in 1986/7.

TEST CAREER

BATTING

M	64
I	96
NO	20
Runs	1,713
HSc	75
Av	22.53
100	–
50	10

BOWLING

Runs	5,646
Wkts	147
Av	38.40
Best	7-78
5w	6
10w	–
Ct	34
St	–

DURING THE 1980s John Emburey was England's premier off-spin bowler, even though he was banished from Test cricket from 1982 to 1985 and again for his part in the visit to South Africa in 1989/90. Were it not for these spells out of the international game he could have played in well over 100 Tests.

Like most young boys, John Emburey just wanted to bowl as fast as he could and this is what he did in the back streets of Peckham. His skill was good enough to get him into the South London Schools Under-10 and 11 sides. But at the age of 12 he accidentally discovered the art of off-spin bowling. Four years later he toured East Africa with the London Schools, going on to play for both England Schools and Surrey Young Cricketers, with whom he toured Canada. In the winter months after his tour to Canada he attended the Surrey nets at Crystal Palace and was desperately keen to join his native county. However, a letter from Arthur McIntyre, the Surrey coach, brought great disappointment, for Surrey had three spinners on the staff already, one of which was Pat Pocock. McIntyre suggested Emburey try Middlesex, but he was so dejected, he didn't even bother. Fortunately for John, McIntyre wrote on his behalf and Don Bennett invited him for a trial at Lord's in mid-season 1971. He impressed sufficiently to be taken on to the staff and made his first-class debut in 1973. Despite some good performances in the 2nd XI his ambitions were frustrated by the presence of Fred Titmus and in six seasons he played no more than a dozen first-class matches for Middlesex. However, his six-year apprenticeship went a long way in helping his first season to be a great success: in just 17 first-class matches he took 81 wickets and was rewarded with his county cap. At the end of the season he went to Australia as part of the Whitbread Scholarship, though there had been rather premature predictions made that he could be picked for England's winter tour of Pakistan and New Zealand. Though he was overlooked for that tour, recognition came with the announcement on his 26th birthday that he would play for England against New Zealand at Lord's in the final Test of the summer of 1978. He made a remarkable start, dismissing Bruce Edgar with his fourth ball.

Over the next few years Emburey emerged as one of the world's leading off-spinners. Under Mike Gatting's forceful captaincy the Ashes series of 1986/7 was won 2–1 in Australia where England also triumphed in two limited-overs competitions. It was a winter of heady success, yet the one Test featuring heroics by John Emburey ended in defeat. The Ashes had been safely retained when the two teams arrived in Sydney for the final Test. Almost 100,000 people turned up to see a game which held the attention up to the penultimate over. Things didn't begin too well for Emburey, as Dean Jones hit 184 not out in Australia's first innings total of 343. England were in dire trouble at 142 for 6 when Emburey came out to bat. Soon he was hobbling with a groin strain but he stayed at the crease for three-and-a-half hours to score 69 and keep England in the hunt. Then came his greatest contribution to a Test match – he wheeled through 46 overs of controlled spin bowling. From 106 for 2, Australia were bowled out for 251 with Emburey responsible for the last seven wickets. A target of 320 was

LEP

undoubtedly stiff but Gatting scored a brave 96 and Emburey batted more than an hour for 22 but he was finally defeated by a grubber with only one over remaining. During the same tour Emburey established a world record by scoring 46 entirely in boundaries for an England XI against Tasmania in Hobart.

After 23 seasons with Middlesex, where he took 1,430 first-class wickets, Emburey had two seasons with Northamptonshire, combining playing with his duties as the county's coach.

Godfrey Evans

Born: 18 August 1920, Finchley, Middlesex
Died: 3 May 1999

TEST CAREER	
BATTING	
M	91
I	133
NO	14
Runs	2,439
HSc	104
Av	20.49
100	2
50	8
Ct	173
St	46

- He did not concede a single bye in his first Test v Australia during a total of 659 off 1,384 balls – still the highest Test total without a bye.
- He established a world first-class record by taking 97 minutes to score his first run in the Adelaide Test of 1946/7.
- He became the second wicket-keeper after W.A.S. Oldfield to make 100 dismissals and complete the 1,000 runs/100 dismissals double, scoring 98 not out before lunch on the third day of the Test against India at Lord's.
- He became the first wicket-keeper to make 200 dismissals and complete the 2,000 runs/200 dismissals double.
- He exceeded 1,000 runs in a season four times.
- He made nine dismissals for Kent v New Zealanders at Canterbury in 1949.

GODFREY EVANS was a brilliant, extrovert wicket-keeper, one of the greatest exponents ever seen. He relished the big occasion and managed to combine acrobatic showmanship with glovework of the highest class.

With a reputation already established as a batsman, Evans joined the Kent staff in 1937. At his trial he was pressed into service as a 'keeper and startled onlookers referred to him as 'another Ames'. Studying both Ames and Kent's other Test wicket-keeper, 'Hopper' Levett, allowed Evans to continue his education behind the stumps while retaining his place as a middle-order batsman. He made his debut against Surrey at Blackheath in July 1939 and a week later took to the field for the first time as a county wicket-keeper. In only the second over a ball from Norman Harding clipped the edge of the bat and jagged down the leg-side – Evans took off and caught it.

The war put paid to his immediate ambition and in June 1940 he joined the Royal Army Service Corps. His breakthrough came in the summer of 1943 when an RAF side captained by former Sussex and England skipper Arthur Gilligan appeared at Aldershot. As well as hitting 37 in even time, Evans executed the leg-side stumping of Glamorgan's Peter Judge. Gilligan described this as 'the best piece of work since the outbreak of war'.

In 1946 Evans returned to Canterbury with much to prove. While Ames decided to concentrate on his batting and Levett returned to the 2nd XI, Evans seized his opportunity with both hands. By July he was representing England in a trial at Canterbury and in August he played in the third Test against India at The Oval. That autumn he set sail to Australia and New Zealand with the MCC party under Wally Hammond and having been omitted from the first disastrous Test at Brisbane, kept his place for a record 27 consecutive matches thereafter.

Evans was dropped in 1949 and 1951 but otherwise represented as near automatic a Test selection as any England player until his retirement in 1959. In 1950 against the combined wiles of Ramadhin and Valentine he scored 104 at Old Trafford. In 1952 he had his most successful season with the bat, scoring a second Test hundred at Lord's (98 of which came before lunch) and making 1,241 runs for the county.

Godfrey Evans had all the qualities of a born wicket-keeper: a superb pair of hands, agility, balance, anticipation and, perhaps most of all, vitality. He was a shrewd tactician, spotting weaknesses in a batsman and passing on the tips to the bowler. However, he was so enthusiastic that he would keep up a non-stop chatter of encouragement to his team-mates, both in the changing-room and on the field of

ES

play. At his very best Evans was capable of making catches and taking stumpings which no other man would have even considered chances. He was superb standing back, good near the stumps and possibly the fastest mover everywhere.

When he did eventually lose his England place, it was not through diminishing form but because of the selectors' need to build a younger side. Although he retired from Kent soon after his last Test in 1959, he was recalled eight years later while Alan Knott was making his England debut and kept with much of his former brilliance.

Evans's subsequent career led him from pub tenancy to public relations. Perhaps his best-known position was as cricket adviser to Ladbrokes, for whom he set the infamous 500–1 odds on the 1981 Test at Headingley.

Keith Fletcher

Born: 20 May 1944, Worcester

- His innings of 178 in 379 minutes averted England's first defeat by New Zealand at Lord's in 1973.
- His 100 in 458 minutes against Pakistan at The Oval in 1974 remains the slowest in English first-class cricket.
- He was the first England captain touring India to put the opposition in to bat first. He won the toss five times in the six-match series.
- He exceeded 1,000 runs in a season 20 times.
- He scored 29,434 runs for Essex.

TEST CAREER

BATTING

M	59
I	96
NO	14
Runs	3,272
HSc	216
Av	39.90
100	7
50	19

BOWLING

Runs	193
Wkts	2
Av	96.50
Best	1-6
5w	–
10w	–
Ct	54
St	–

AN EXCITING and talented middle-order batsman, Keith Fletcher possessed a complete repertoire of strokes and was capable of taking an attack apart.

When he arrived to join the Essex staff, some of the players practising close catching noticed his long and rather pointed shoes, promptly nicknaming him the 'Gnome'. Fletcher made his Essex debut in 1962, having seen only one first-class match. The following season he scored 1,310 runs and was awarded his county cap, although the undoubted potential of his cricket had yet to be fulfilled.

His maiden century came in 1964 when he hit an unbeaten 103 against Lancashire at Old Trafford, quickly followed by 125 in Essex's victory over the touring Australians at Southend. In 1965 he totalled 1,486 runs, while the following summer he scored 1,550 runs, among them a superb 106 against the West Indies, in which he picked up a glorious six down the leg-side off Wes Hall to take him to his hundred. Also in that summer he took 42 catches, breaking his own record from the previous season.

He hit the highest score of his career – 228 not out against Sussex at Hastings – in 1968, an innings that gained him his first England cap. His England debut came at Headingley that summer and for the wrong reasons. He had been named in the England XII but it was not expected that he would play. However, Tom Graveney cut his hand opening a can of food and Yorkshire's Phil Sharpe, who had not even been in the original squad, was called up as standby. It was quite natural that Fletcher should play but of course the Yorkshire crowd saw it differently: they thought Sharpe should play and when Fletcher dropped three catches and failed to score, the Leeds crowd never let up.

After finishing second to Geoff Boycott in the national batting averages of 1971, Fletcher had an outstanding season the following summer and it amazed most Essex followers that he was only chosen for one Test.

LEP

Author

At the end of the 1975 season Fletcher was appointed captain of Essex in succession to Brian Taylor. A firm disciplinarian, he earned great respect from the players because of his natural ability and he ended his first season in charge as one of *Wisden*'s Five Cricketers of the Year.

His appearances in the England side meant frequent absences from Essex and his century against Pakistan at The Oval in 1974 still remains the slowest in English first-class cricket at 458 minutes.

In 1979 Fletcher led Essex to the County Championship title for the first time in their history. His leadership qualities prompted the England Committee to name him captain of the England party to tour India and Sri Lanka in 1981/2. Keith Fletcher was the only England captain to win the toss five times in a six-Test series and the first England captain to put the opposition in first in India. He played in 59 Tests for England, 7 of them as captain. He hit 7 centuries, the highest of them being 216 against New Zealand at Auckland in 1974/5 but probably his best Test innings was the 170 also made against New Zealand at Lord's in 1973.

In 1985 Fletcher was invited to Buckingham Palace to receive the OBE from the Queen. It was an honour thoroughly and richly deserved, reflecting the fortunes of both the man and the county club. By the end of the 1985 season he had become the first captain to lead a county side to the game's four major honours. He is now the club's cricket consultant and there have been few greater servants to Essex than the 'Gnome'.

Angus Fraser

Born: 8 August 1965, Billinge, Lancashire

- His best bowling in Test matches is 8 for 53 v West Indies at Port-of-Spain in 1997/8 – the record England innings analysis against the West Indies.
- He was a *Wisden* Cricketer of the Year in 1995.
- He was made an MBE in 1999.
- He was appointed captain of Middlesex in 2001.

TEST CAREER

BATTING

M	46
I	67
NO	15
Runs	388
HSc	32
Av	7.46
100	–
50	–

BOWLING

Runs	4,836
Wkts	177
Av	27.32
Best	8-53
5w	13
10w	2
Ct	9
St	–

THOUGH HE WAS born in Billinge, deep in Rugby League country between Wigan and St Helens, Angus Fraser moved south and began his career with Stanmore, a longtime nursery for the Middlesex team. Fraser proceeded serenely through the Middlesex Schools XI and the county's Young Cricketers before making his first-team debut in 1984.

The wider world first caught sight of Angus Fraser in the third Ashes Test of 1989 at Edgbaston. He came on first change after Graham Dilley and Paul Jarvis. At once the appealingly solemn young man took a notable first wicket: he clean bowled

LEP

Steve Waugh – the Australian's first Test dismissal in England after 584 deliveries and 393 runs. It was an illustrious first scalp and Fraser's match figures of 33-8-63-4 gave notice at once that he was likely to be a fixture for England all through the next decade.

In the Caribbean during the winter months Fraser found himself the second most experienced bowler after Gladstone Small. In his 11 overs before lunch on the first day of the opening Test at Sabina Park he conceded only 11 runs. After Small and Capel had nipped in to pick up Haynes, Richardson and Best, Fraser came back to greet the mighty Viv Richards, with a lifting fizzer which Russell held but the umpire refused to uphold. Malcolm eventually dismissed Richards, while Fraser clinically polished off the innings with five wickets for six runs in only six overs. Fraser took five more wickets in the Trinidad Test before a rib injury not only put him out of the tour but forced him to miss half the following season and the three-Test series against New Zealand.

After a successful series against India, Fraser went to Australia in 1990/1, lauded as an Ashes trump card, but in the match against Western Australia he began to feel an ache in his right hip. He played through it and a month down the line in the Christmas Test at the MCG he bowled 59 overs and took 7 wickets. He missed the Sydney Test but played at Adelaide, after which he flew home early, dosed with cortisone and despair. After differing prognoses, surgery, recuperation, more surgery and more recuperation, a Cambridge surgeon did the trick.

His return to the Test side came against Australia at The Oval in 1993 – two and a half years after his previous international appearance. Though England had already lost the rubber, Fraser's eight

wickets won him the man-of-the-match award and a place on the West Indies tour. That summer he had produced his best figures in the County Championship with 7 for 40 against Leicestershire but in Barbados in April 1994 he capped his previous record with 8 for 75, the best for England anywhere since Bob Willis at Headingley in 1981.

Thereafter he was in and out of the side, and with Ray Illingworth as Chairman of Selectors he was surprisingly overlooked for the Ashes tour in 1994/5 though he was later flown out as a replacement. In 1995 Fraser finished the series against the West Indies with 16 wickets, twice as many as anyone but Cork. He did not feature in 1996 and the Ashes summer the following year passed him by: he was looking very much 'a former England player'. However, he was recalled for the West Indies tour in 1997/8, returning triumphant: he took 27 wickets at 18.22 including 8 for 53 at Port-of-Spain, the best figures ever recorded by an England bowler against the West Indies. Against South Africa in 1998 Fraser took 24 wickets, by far the most for England, at 20.50.

He announced his retirement in 2002.

Mike Gatting

Born: 6 June 1957, Kingsbury, Middlesex

- When he scored 207 against India at Madras in 1984/5, he completed the first instance of 2 double hundreds in an England innings – Graeme Fowler (201) was the other batsman.
- In 1986/7 he became the third England captain to regain the Ashes in Australia.
- He captained Middlesex from 1983 to 1997.
- He exceeded 1,000 runs 19 times and in 1984 he headed the national batting averages with 2,257 runs at 68.39.

TEST CAREER	
BATTING	
M	79
I	138
NO	14
Runs	4,409
HSc	207
Av	35.55
100	10
50	21
BOWLING	
Runs	317
Wkts	4
Av	79.25
Best	1-14
5w	–
10w	–
Ct	59
St	–

A BOLD, EXCITING and pugnacious batsman, Mike Gatting's approach to both county and Test cricket changed little from his club cricket days with Brondesbury.

He played cricket for Middlesex Under-15s for two seasons and hit a century for England Schools in their match against the Public Schools in 1973. In 1974 he represented England Young Cricketers and became a scholarship boy with the Cricket Society. He later went on a Whitbread Scholarship to Australia. There were no other distractions for Mike Gatting, except possibly one – he won a bronze medal along with his brother Steve (a professional footballer) at Neasden Ritz for ballroom dancing.

Middlesex captain Mike Brearley had great confidence in Gatting's ability. In his first full season with the county, 1977, he hit 1,095 runs and was awarded his county cap. Gatting made his Test debut in Pakistan in 1977/8 but it took him 54 innings to register his first three-figure score for England (achieved during the first Test in India at Bombay in 1984/5). Three innings later he scored a magnificent 207, sharing in the highest-ever second-wicket partnership for England with Graeme Fowler.

He succeeded Mike Brearley as captain of Middlesex in 1983 and although Gatting had lost his place in the England side against West Indies in the preceding series, he was named as vice-captain to David Gower for the 1984/5 tour of India. When Gower fell out of favour after defeat in the first Test by India in 1986, Gatting was made captain. He lost the series against India and the one against New Zealand that followed but in 1986/7 he led England on arguably the most successful tour ever of Australia, winning the Test series, the Perth Challenge and the World Series Cup. He also took England to the World Cup Final in 1987. However, the same final saw him pilloried for his dismissal to a reverse sweep at a crucial period in the match. Worse followed on the Pakistan tour that winter: Gatting and Shakoor Rana were involved in the most controversial cricket incident since the 'Bodyline' series. The following season he was relieved of the England captaincy after the so-called 'barmaid scandal' despite the England Committee's apparent acceptance of his denial of involvement. Then in 1989 Gatting and fifteen others took the decision to go to South Africa during the Australian Test series and were consequently banned from international cricket for five years.

On the domestic front, Gatting rose to the challenge of captaining Middlesex. There were certain things in his favour when he took over: he inherited a good side who had been used to winning; he was well respected by his colleagues; and the Middlesex Committee were fully behind him. In his first season in charge, he topped the batting averages with 1,373 runs at 72.26 and was named as one of *Wisden*'s Five Cricketers of the Year. The following summer he topped 3,000 runs and hit the highest score of his career, 258 against Somerset at Bath. Under his captaincy Middlesex won the County Championship in 1985, 1990 and 1993, the NatWest Trophy in 1984 and 1988, the Benson & Hedges Cup in 1983 and 1986 and the Sunday League in 1992.

Gatting was quite a formidable sight on his way to the wicket: the swirling of the arms and bat on arrival at the crease, a most emphatic stance. In recent decades he was one of only three English-born batsmen – along with Graham Gooch and Ian Botham – capable of completely destroying the opposition attack.

Graham Gooch

Born: 23 July 1953, Leytonstone, Essex

- He established an Essex first-class record of 2,559 runs in 1984.
- He captained Essex in 1986/7 and from 1989 to 1994.
- He is the leading Essex run-getter of all-time with 30,701 at an average of 51.77.
- In 1989 he ended the season with the highest Sunday League average of 95.66.
- In 1990 he topped the national batting averages, scoring 2,746 runs at 101.70, including a dozen centuries.
- He holds the record for the highest score in the Benson & Hedges Cup with 198 not out v Sussex at Hove in 1982.
- In 1990 in the Lord's Test against India he scored 333 in the first innings and 123 in the second – the first batsman to complete such a feat.
- He was made an OBE in 1991.

TEST CAREER

BATTING

M	118
I	215
NO	6
Runs	8,900
HSc	333
Av	42.58
100	20
50	46

BOWLING

Runs	1,069
Wkts	23
Av	46.47
Best	3-39
5w	–
10w	–
Ct	103
St	–

WHEN GRAHAM GOOCH was appointed captain of England against the West Indies at The Oval in the summer of 1988 he became England's fourth captain of the series. By that time he had become his country's leading batsman, although his start in Test cricket had been inauspicious.

He made his Essex debut in 1973, hitting the first of 94 centuries for the county the following summer against Leicestershire. He was soon seen as a very powerful and aggressive batsman and in 1975 was called into the Test side a little prematurely, making his debut against the pace of Lillee and Thomson at Edgbaston. Despite making 0 and 0, he was retained for the second Test at Lord's but then

disappeared from Test cricket until 1978 when he returned against Pakistan as Geoff Boycott's opening partner.

When Essex won the County Championship in 1979 Gooch gave the team an attacking look right from the start. In the Benson & Hedges final against Surrey he played a magnificent innings of 120 in the first of a run of successes in Lord's finals.

In 1979/80, still seeking that elusive first Test century, he was run out for 99 at Melbourne. Gooch's first Test century came at Lord's against West Indies in 1980 when he scored a magnificent 123 out of the first 165 runs. In 1980/1 he toured the West Indies and was by far the most successful of the English batsmen, scoring 116 at Bridgetown and 153 at Kingston to average 57.50 in the series. Following the tour of India and Sri Lanka in 1981/2, he captained a rebel tour of South Africa and was banned from Test cricket for three years.

In 1982 in the Benson & Hedges Cup zonal match at Hove, Gooch hit the Sussex attack for 198 not out – the highest score made in a one-

LEP

day competition in England. His batting in 1984 was absolutely brilliant: he became the first man that season to reach 2,000 runs, scoring 2,559, the highest by an Essex player in a season.

He returned to the England side in 1985 and hit 196 at The Oval as England won the series against Australia. He became captain of Essex in 1986 but despite leading the county to their third Championship title in four years, he relinquished the post after a couple of seasons because he felt his form was adversely affected. He was reappointed in 1989 by which time he had led England against West Indies and Sri Lanka. He had been named as captain of England for the trip to India in 1988/9 but the tour was cancelled because of the South African connections of Gooch and other members of the party. Gooch became a national hero when he led England to victory over West Indies at Kingston in 1989/90 and he came close to leading the team to victory at Port-of-Spain where he himself was forced to retire hurt with a broken finger. The year 1990 belonged to Graham Gooch. He hit 154 as England beat New Zealand at Edgbaston and followed this with innings of 333 and 123 in the victory over India at Lord's. His triple century was the highest innings ever played by an England captain.

A useful if under-used seam bowler and a fine slip fielder, Gooch changed his batting style over the years, adding a watchful defence to his strength and belligerence. Capable of the destruction of any attack, Gooch lifted the spirits of English cricket by his own supreme example after a few years of unhappiness and controversy. When he retired from first-class cricket in 1997 he was both England's and Essex's leading run-getter of all time.

Darren Gough

Born: 18 September 1970, Barnsley, Yorkshire

- He took four wickets in five balls (including the hat trick) for Yorkshire v Kent at Headingley in 1995.
- His best bowling figures of 7 for 28 came in the Roses match at Headingley, also in 1995.
- He was named one of *Wisden*'s Five Cricketers of the Year in 1998.
- He performed the hat trick against Australia at Sydney in 1998/9 – the first for England in an Ashes series since 1899.

TEST CAREER

BATTING

M	56
I	83
NO	18
Runs	806
HSc	65
Av	12.40
100	–
50	2

BOWLING

Runs	6,288
Wkts	228
Av	27.57
Best	6-42
5w	9
10w	–
Ct	12
St	–

FROM HIS comprehensive school background in Barnsley, Darren Gough aspired to earn his living from sport. A brief flirtation with Rotherham United FC ended when he was offered a YTS place on the Yorkshire staff at 17. He made his first-class debut at Lord's in April 1989 – the first product of Yorkshire's cricket school to appear in the County Championship. He made a startling entry: the wicket of former England captain Mike Gatting was one of five the teenager claimed in the match. However, after this remarkable start, a back injury ruined the rest of his season and Gough didn't return until the end of August. The next three seasons rarely hinted that

he would become a consistently accurate quick bowler but in 1993 his off-cutter developed and he also began to bowl the yorker with devastating effect. That season he took 55 wickets at an average of 25.74 and produced his best figures in the County Championship with 7 for 42 (10 for 96 in the match) against Somerset at Taunton. It was an eventful year: he was selected to go to Holland with an England XI, chosen as Whittingdale Young Cricketer of the Month in July and awarded his county cap in September because of his success with the ball.

Gough always possessed the ability to bowl fast but in his early years at Yorkshire he became frustrated by his tendency to bowl two four-balls an over and toyed with trying a tight line and cutting his pace. Thankfully he pulled back from the charge.

In 1994 he played in a one-day international against New Zealand. His debut was encouraging – two wickets, including Martin Crowe's, in his first over and an invigorating display of quick bowling had him hailed as England's new fast bowling hero. Unfortunately his hopes of immediate Test match recognition were dashed by a nipped side muscle which incapacitated him for four weeks. When he did make his Test debut at Old Trafford, he revived England's innings with a lusty 65.

In 1995 Gough took four wickets in five balls, including a hat trick, in the match against Kent at Headingley and followed this with his best figures of 7 for 28 (10 for 80 in the match) against Lancashire in a non-Championship fixture at Headingley. The following summer he not only had his

LEP

LEP

best season with the ball, taking 66 wickets at 22.69 runs apiece, but also scored his maiden first-class century with a knock of 121 against Warwickshire at Headingley.

At Test level, Gough's best figures with the ball came in front of his home crowd at Headingley in 1998 when he took 6 for 42 against South Africa, helping England to a surprise 2–1 series win. On the 1998/9 tour of Australia, Gough performed the hat trick for the first time for England in the Sydney test.

He played in two World Cups but was sidelined for the entire series against New Zealand in 1999 because of a career-threatening calf injury.

Passionately committed even in the bleakest of situations, he was named man-of-the-series against the West Indies in 2000 thanks to a haul of 25 wickets that included Brian Lara's scalp on five occasions. With the bat he was Dominic Cork's foil during England's dramatic two wicket win at Lord's.

During the course of 2001's Ashes series, he became only the eighth English bowler to reach 200 Test victims. As England's premier strike bowler, he has the potential to add to this total over the coming years.

David Gower

Born: 1 April 1957, Tunbridge Wells, Kent

- His innings of 215 is the highest score v Australia at Edgbaston and the second highest by an England captain v Australia anywhere.
- He captained Leicestershire from 1984 to 1986 and again in 1988 and 1989, and Hampshire in 1990.
- He was named a *Wisden* Cricketer of the Year and the Young Cricketer of the Year in 1978.
- He was made an OBE in 1992.
- He exceeded 1,000 runs in a season 13 times.

TEST CAREER	
BATTING	
M	117
I	204
NO	18
Runs	8,231
HSc	215
Av	44.25
100	18
50	39
BOWLING	
Runs	20
Wkts	1
Av	20.00
Best	1-1
5w	–
10w	–
Ct	74
St	–

DAVID GOWER has been described as the most accomplished English batsman of his generation and his languid, graceful style has been likened to that of Frank Woolley, another great left-hander born in Kent. Though he spent his early years in Tanganyika where his father served in the Colonial Office, he returned to English shores to develop his cricket talent at King's School, Canterbury.

After being recommended to Leicestershire, he made his first-class debut in 1975, the season the county went on to win the Championship for the first time in their

96-year history. He toured South Africa with English Schools and West Indies with England's Young Cricketers but drifted into a professional cricket career partly because he was bored with his law studies.

Gower struggled to score runs in 1977 but was picked for the Prudential Trophy matches against Pakistan in 1978 and made 114 not out at The Oval. This performance earned him a Test place at Edgbaston where he hit his first ball for four and went on to 58. Later that season he made his first Test century at The Oval against New Zealand. In 1978/9 he made his first century against Australia at Perth and when India visited England in 1979, he hit 200 not out in the first Test at Edgbaston for six years.

There followed a lean period which culminated in him being dropped after the first Test against the West Indies in 1980. He toured the Caribbean the following winter, however, and in an otherwise disappointing series came back to form with 154 not out in Kingston. He was still not fulfilling potential when he toured Australia in 1982/3 but in the World Series Cup, a bonanza of one-day matches which followed the Test series, he made three centuries against New Zealand. Having made over 1,000 runs in five Tests and ten WSC matches, he was named Benson & Hedges International Cricketer of the Year. More valuable runs came in the New Zealand tour to England in 1983 when he scored two centuries in a series for the first time.

LEP

The feat was repeated in Pakistan in 1983/4 after he took over the England captaincy when Willis was forced to return home. He perhaps regretted his responsibilities in his first full series in charge: the West Indies beat England 5–0 in 1984 – the worst defeat ever inflicted on England. However, he kept the job and in India in 1984/5 he led with tact and shrewdness through a most difficult time which saw the assassination of the Indian Prime Minister Mrs Gandhi and of Percy Norris, the British Deputy High Commissioner. England lost the first Test but won the series, not least because of Gower's calm and control.

In 1985 Gower regained the Ashes from an Australian side weakened by the defections to a rebel tour of South Africa. In the third Test at Trent Bridge he made his first century as England captain. In the fifth Test at Edgbaston he hit his highest-ever test score of 215 and in the sixth, 1,157. He scored 732 runs in the series at an average of 81.33.

A poor tour of the West Indies in 1985/6, when his captaincy was criticised as being too lenient, and a bad start to the home series with India led to his replacement as captain by Gatting. However, when Ted Dexter took over as England's Chairman of Selectors, Gower was reinstated as captain for the series against Australia in 1989. After a heavy defeat Gower was not only deprived of the captaincy for the tour of the West Indies but was not even selected for the trip. In 1990 he won back a place in the England side for the three Tests against India and hit a century at The Oval. He joined Gooch's team to go to Australia and made two centuries that series but was guilty of a breach of discipline with an ill-judged flying escapade.

On leaving Leicestershire, he joined Hampshire but he never seemed to have a great appetite for the county game. There is little doubt that he should have been an Edwardian amateur for he would have graced the golden age.

Tom Graveney

Born: 16 June 1927, Riding Mill, Northumberland

- He exceeded 1,000 runs in a season 20 times (plus twice on tour), including 2,000 runs on seven occasions.
- In 1964 he became the 15th batsman to score 100 first-class hundreds, his final tally of 122 including seven double centuries.
- He is the only player to score 10,000 runs for two counties and the first with an entirely post-war career to score either 30,000 runs or 100 hundreds.
- He scored 100 in each innings of a match on four occasions.
- His fourth-wicket stand of 402 with Willie Watson for MCC v British Guyana at Georgetown in 1953/4 remains the record for any wicket by an English touring team.
- He scored 200 of Gloucestershire's 298 v Glamorgan at Newport in 1956 – the lowest completed total to include a double century.

TEST CAREER	
BATTING	
M	79
I	123
NO	13
Runs	4,882
HSc	258
Av	44.38
100	11
50	20
BOWLING	
Runs	167
Wkts	1
Av	167.00
Best	1-34
5w	–
10w	–
Ct	80
St	–

TOM GRAVENEY had a natural talent for the game of cricket and this, plus a recommendation from his elder brother Ken who was already on the Gloucestershire staff, brought him to Bristol. While he was on leave from his post in the Army as a PT Instructor in the Middle East, he turned out in some benefit games for Gloucestershire. In these matches he opened the

batting and Billy Neale was so impressed with the young Graveney's technique that he put in a good word for him with the Gloucestershire committee.

Towards the end of his first season in the Gloucestershire side, Graveney, who had by now completed his National Service, was awarded his county cap by the then captain, Basil Allen. In front of the entire Gloucestershire squad Allen threw his cap across the dressing-room saying, 'You'd better have this. You'd have got it much sooner if you weren't so big headed!' Allen was a great believer in keeping professional newcomers firmly in their place! Graveney was soon established as the most promising young batsman in the country.

In 1951 Graveney scored 2,291 runs, his best performance coming in the match against Northamptonshire at Bristol when he hit 103 and 105 not out. In 1951/2 he was England's number 3 on the tour to India, Pakistan and Sri Lanka, his aggregate total of 1,393 runs including six centuries. The following season Graveney scored 2,066 runs and was selected as one of *Wisden*'s Cricketers of the Year. In 1953/4 he represented the MCC in their fixture against British Guyana at Georgetown.

He scored 231 as he and Willie Watson added 402 for the fourth wicket – still a record for any English touring team. The following summer he hit 222 against Derbyshire at Chesterfield; it was his highest score for Gloucestershire. In 1956 he topped the county's averages, scoring 2,397 runs. In the

LEP

match against Essex he produced a remarkable achievement, scoring more than half his team's total in both innings of the match – 100 out of 153 and then 67 out of 107. Also that season against Glamorgan at Newport, Graveney scored a magnificent 200 out of his side's total of 298. His runs were scored on a turning wicket against the spin of Jim McConnon and Don Shepherd.

Though he'd made his Test debut in 1951, it was 1957 before Graveney won a regular place in the side. He hammered the West Indian bowlers all round Trent Bridge, scoring a glorious 258 in the process. He followed up later in the series with 164 at The Oval, while on the county circuit he hit hundreds in each innings of the match against Warwickshire.

He played for Gloucestershire for twelve years and was their captain for the last two, leading them to the runners-up spot in the County Championship in 1959. By the time 1960 came round the Gloucestershire committee couldn't make up its mind whether or not it wanted an amateur or professional captain and because some members were critical of his leadership style, Graveney was relieved of the captaincy. Having scored 19,705 runs at an average of 43.02, Graveney left to play for Worcestershire. At New Road he improved as a player, helping his new county win the Championship in 1964 and 1965, scoring 2,385 runs and 1,768 runs respectively.

Graveney played all his strokes with elegance, perfect timing and style, and is the only cricketer to score more than 10,000 runs for two different counties. In the 1968 New Year's Honours List he was made an OBE for his services to cricket.

During the early part of his career some selectors and Test captains wondered whether Graveney had the right temperament to succeed at the highest level. His 79 Test appearances, 4,882 runs, 11 centuries and average of 44.38 show nobody need have worried.

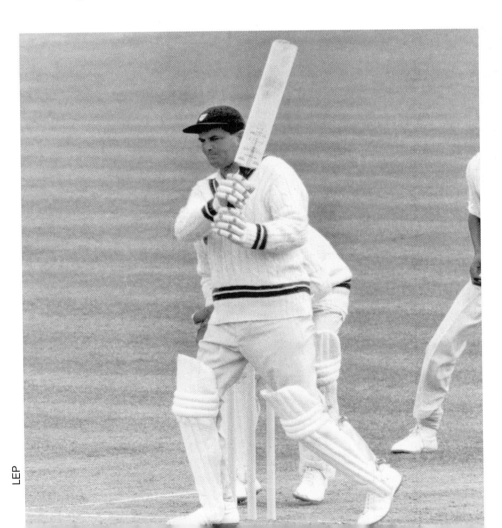

LEP

Tony Greig

Born: 6 October 1946, Queenstown, South Africa

- He was the first player to score 100 and take 5 wickets in an innings of the same Test for England, doing so against West Indies at Bridgetown in 1973/4.
- He emulated Wilfred Rhodes and Trevor Bailey by scoring 2,000 runs and taking 100 wickets for England.
- He was the first to score 3,000 runs and take 100 wickets for England.
- He exceeded 1,000 runs in a season seven times (plus once on tour).
- He performed the hat trick for Eastern Province v Natal at Port Elizabeth in 1971/2.

TEST CAREER	
BATTING	
M	58
I	93
NO	4
Runs	3,599
HSc	148
Av	40.43
100	8
50	20
BOWLING	
Runs	4,541
Wkts	141
Av	32.20
Best	8-86
5w	6
10w	2
Ct	87
St	–

HIS SCOTTISH FATHER having gone to South Africa with the RAF during the Second World War to train pilots, Tony Greig made his first-class debut for Border in 1965/6.

Greig joined Sussex in 1966 and made his county debut in May 1967 against Lancashire at Hove. Already standing an impressive 6ft 8in, slim and blond, the 20-year-old Greig saved Sussex with 156 in his first match and it was clear a new star had risen. He scored 1,299 runs and took 67 wickets in his first season. In 1970

Greig played for the England XI against the Rest of the World in the series arranged, ironically, after the cancellation of South Africa's tour.

He made his Test debut in 1972 against Australia and was top-scorer in both innings with 57 and 62 and took five wickets in an England victory. The following winter he toured India where he was a very popular figure and in the fifth Test he made his first Test century, with a total of 148, and shared in a record fifth-wicket stand for England of 254 with Keith Fletcher. In 1973/4 he had an extremely successful tour of West Indies where his competitiveness got him into trouble in the first Test at Port-of-Spain. On the last ball of the second day Julien played the ball back down the pitch and Greig, seeing Kallicharran out of his ground, threw down the wicket. Kallicharran, who was only making his way back to the pavilion, was given out. It took an off-the-field agreement between captain, umpires and officials to reinstate Kallicharran and possibly prevent uproar the following day. Apart from two centuries, Greig played a major part in England making a draw of this series when, in the final Test, he changed his bowling style from medium swing and seam to off-breaks. He took 8 for 86 and 5 for 70, the best figures at that time produced by an England bowler against West Indies.

When Lillee and Thomson established a superiority over England in the 1974/5 series in Australia, Greig did not flinch against their awesome and dangerous speed, and his innings of 110 at Brisbane

LEP

was a courageous knock which held England together. In 1975 Greig became England captain when Denness stood down after the first Test against Australia.

In 1976 the West Indies were the visitors and Greig made a combative but ill-considered remark about making them grovel: in the event, the West Indian fast bowlers were merciless in inflicting a 3–0 defeat.

Greig's style of inspirational leadership was beginning to weld a more successful England side, however, and the tour of India in 1976/7 was a triumph – India lost the first three Tests to a touring side for the first time ever. Then Greig's role in World Series Cricket became known. The immediate result was the loss of the England captaincy to Brearley, his vice-captain in India. Greig was never forgiven by the establishment and within a couple of years his first-class career had ended. He became managing director of an insurance company set up by Kerry Packer and one of the cricket presenters on Channel 9 television.

Throughout his career Greig fought against epilepsy. For a while he was England's shining knight. During the Packer affair, he was articulate, polite and reasonable in his assertions that all was for the best as far as the welfare of cricketers was concerned, a claim that bears examination now the dust has settled. Tony Greig deserves to be remembered not as a player who vaguely besmirched the name of cricket, as some traditionalists would like to have it, but as one of England's best captains and all-rounders.

Graeme Hick

Born: 23 May 1966, Salisbury, Rhodesia

- He was named a *Wisden* Cricketer of the Year in 1986 when he became the youngest ever to score 2,000 runs in a season.
- During the course of that season he scored 1,019 runs before the end of June, including a record 410 runs in April.
- He has exceeded 1,000 runs 16 times with a best of 2,713 in 1988.
- He scored 405 not out against Somerset at Taunton in 1988 – a Worcestershire record and then the second highest in matches in this country.
- He scored 645 runs without being dismissed in 1990, a UK record.
- At 32 he became the second youngest player to score 100 first-class hundreds.
- He was made captain of Worcestershire in 2000.

TEST CAREER

BATTING

M	65
I	114
NO	6
Runs	3,383
HSc	178
Av	31.32
100	6
50	18

BOWLING

Runs	1,306
Wkts	23
Av	56.78
Best	4-126
5w	–
10w	–
Ct	90
St	–

GRAEME HICK has been the enigma of English cricket for the last decade. The man everyone expected to become England's best batsman of recent years never quite scaled the heights that were forecast.

Hick was a good batsman from the beginning, scoring a century for his junior school team when he was only six. He came to England with the Zimbabwe squad for the Prudential

LEP

World Cup in England when he was only 17 but did not play. He returned to England in 1984, however, to play in the Birmingham League and for Worcestershire 2nd XI. Hick soon made a mark for Kidderminster in an innings of 182 not out – the highest in the Birmingham League for 44 years – and his 1,234 runs in a season were a record. In the last match of the 1984 season he made his debut for Worcestershire against Surrey at The Oval. In 1985 Hick scored 1,265 first-class runs at an average of 52.70. He played for Zimbabwe in a short tour of England and made 230 against Oxford University. Hick then decided to withdraw from the Zimbabwe side for the ICC Trophy to begin the long qualification for England. 1986 was his first full season for Worcestershire. He soon showed his power by smashing 227 not out in the second innings against title-chasing Nottinghamshire. In the next match he scored 219 against Glamorgan, including 188 between lunch and tea on the second day, and in a run-chase second innings he hit 52 off 22 balls to ensure the win. In this match Hick became the first player to 1,000 runs that season and in the return in September another match-winning knock saw him hit 107 off 121 balls to become the youngest player ever to score 2,000 runs in a season. He was 20, had made 2,004 runs at an average of 64.64 and was named as one of *Wisden*'s Five Cricketers of the Year.

In 1988 Hick produced one of the most amazing batting performances seen in English cricket for many years. At Taunton against Somerset he came in with the score at 78 for 1, which soon deteriorated to 132 for 5. But by the close the total had climbed to 312 – Hick 179 not out – and by

LEP

the time Rhodes went the next day for 56 the pair had added a county record of 265 for the sixth wicket. Hick was 257 at lunch on the second day and between lunch and tea, when the innings was declared, he went to 405, sharing a new county eighth-wicket record with Richard Illingworth of 177 unparted. His innings is the second highest in England behind Archie MacLaren's 424 in 1895, also made against Somerset at Taunton. His overall aggregate for the season of 2,713 runs gave him an average of 77.51, effectively top of the national averages. His ten centuries equalled the Worcestershire record. In 1990 Hick became the quickest to reach 10,000 runs in county cricket from just 179 innings.

Hick finally qualified for England in 1991 and no player since the Second World War had come to the Test side with better credentials. But it took him eight Tests to score his first fifty and his first Test century against India (178 at Bombay) was achieved on his 22nd appearance.

Over the years, we have been told that Graeme Hick cannot play pace. This is a piece of received wisdom originating from his initial Test failures against the West Indies. Given the weight of expectation at the start of that series, it is hardly surprising that theories about Hick's technical competence should abound. Yet anyone who has seen Graeme Hick taking hundreds off Waqar Younis, Allan Donald or Franklyn Stephenson, or his magnificent innings against the West Indians at Worcester in 1988, will tell you that he does not lack bottle. There seems to be a tendency in English cricket that when a player is super-talented, any flaw in his game is magnified and exaggerated until everyone considers it to be serious enough to warrant his exclusion.

Nasser Hussain

Born: 28 March 1968, Madras, India

- Named Young Cricketer of the Year in 1989.
- He has exceeded 1,000 runs five times with a best of 1,854 in 1995.
- Captain of Essex in 1999 and club captain from 2000 to date.
- He scored 207 against Australia at Edgbaston in 1997.
- He was made England captain in 1999.

TEST CAREER	
BATTING	
M	69
I	124
NO	13
Runs	4,006
HSc	207
Av	36.09
100	10
50	21
BOWLING	
Runs	16
Wkts	0
Av	–
Best	–
5w	–
10w	–
Ct	48
St	–

NASSER HUSSAIN first came to the fore after several impressive performances in youth cricket when he was selected to tour Sri Lanka with the Young England team. He had a most successful tour, saving his best for the second four-day 'Test' when he scored 170. Over the next couple of years Indian-born Hussain mixed second-team cricket at Essex with his education at Durham University before making his first-class debut for the county in 1987.

The following season Essex captain Keith Fletcher left himself out of the side in favour of the 20-year-old Hussain who did not let anyone down, scoring 469 runs at an average of 58.62, including an unbeaten 165 against Leicestershire at Chelmsford.

In 1989 Hussain represented the Combined Universities in their marvellous Benson & Hedges Cup run, his 118 in the quarter-final at Taunton taking his side to within three runs of what would have been a remarkable victory. When he rejoined Essex he immediately enhanced his reputation, ending the season with 990 runs at an average of 47.14 and a place in the squad for the final Test match against Australia at The Oval. In 1990 Hussain made his highest score for Essex – 197 against Surrey at The Oval – and although he went on to take various county attacks apart, it was the summer of 1995 before he topped the Essex batting averages.

He made his England debut in February 1990 against the West Indies at Sabina Park, scoring 100 runs in each of the three Tests he played. During the course of these innings, he showed enough glimpses of a steely temperament to suggest a long Test career. Yet he had to wait until 1993 for another chance. After four Tests against the Australians and another Caribbean tour, he did not make a return to the international arena until three years later. But on the England 'A' tour of Pakistan in 1995 Hussain was captain and scored 1,854 runs at an average of 54.75.

At Edgbaston in 1997 he scored a career-best 207 as England opened the Ashes series with a nine-wicket win. He finished the rubber with 431 runs at an average of 39.18. The following summer he became vice-captain and after the World Cup of 1999 took over as skipper when he joined forces with Duncan Fletcher for the series against New Zealand. Despite losses against the Kiwis and South Africa, England went on to record four victories on the bounce against Zimbabwe, West Indies (England's first series success since 1969), Pakistan and Sri Lanka.

In his early days on the international scene Hussain showed signs of temperamental instability but after he took over the captaincy all such traces disappeared. Even as a victim of some poor umpiring decisions in recent seasons, Hussain, who has a reputation as glowing as any England captain since Mike Brearley, has remained calm. The dignity with which he has suffered personal injustice at the hands of umpires has only helped to strengthen his leadership skills.

Despite an Ashes defeat and a 1–0 defeat in India in 2001, Nasser Hussain's England are once again beginning to make their mark in the game, though to be fair, his immediate predecessors, Gooch and Atherton, had none of the back-up Hussain now receives from the England Cricket Board. The new system of central contracts guarantees that outstanding players can be available and fresh throughout the series.

Made an OBE in the New Year's Honours List in 2002, Nasser Hussain has intimated that he will stand down after the 2003 World Cup. Let's hope he can be persuaded to change his mind.

Len Hutton

Born: 23 June 1916, Fulneck, Pudsey, Yorkshire
Died: 6 September 1990

- His score of 364 against Australia at The Oval in 1938 made in 13 hours and 17 minutes is the longest innings in English first-class cricket. It remains an England record and was a world record until 1958. It remains the highest score at The Oval and by a number 1 batsman in Tests.
- In the match against South Africa at Johannesburg in 1948/9 he shared in a stand of 359 with Cyril Washbrook. It remains England's highest opening stand in all Tests.
- He is the only England batsman to carry his bat twice throughout a complete Test innings.
- In the series against Australia in 1953 he became the first captain to win a rubber after losing the toss in all five Tests.
- He exceeded 1,000 runs in a season 12 times (plus five times on tour) including 3,429 runs in 1949 and 2,000 on eight other occasions.
- He scored 100 first-class centuries in 619 innings, then the fewest innings taken by an Englishman to reach this mark.
- He was the first professional to be elected to honorary membership of the MCC before his career had ended.
- He was knighted for his services to cricket in 1956.

TEST CAREER

BATTING

M	79
I	138
NO	15
Runs	6,971
HSc	364
Av	56.67
100	19
50	33

BOWLING

Runs	232
Wkts	3
Av	77.33
Best	1-2
5w	–
10w	–
Ct	57
St	–

LEN HUTTON won recognition as one of the greatest batsmen in cricket history through many prodigious feats, one of the earliest being his 364 in The Oval Test of 1938. It was the longest innings and the highest Test total up to that time and it remains the highest innings played in an Ashes series. Yet probably his most remarkable achievement was resuming his career for Yorkshire and England with no loss of skill after the Second World War: an accident in an Army gymnasium meant his left arm was now shorter and less strong than his right.

Hutton's early years with the Yorkshire 2nd XI left little doubt that another great England batsman had emerged, though few perhaps guessed that in a country where batsmen generally mature late, his impact would come so soon. He played in his first first-class match for Yorkshire at Cambridge in 1934 but failed to score, just as he was to do in his first Test only three years later. Yorkshire used him sparingly but awarded him his county cap in his third season when he made 1,000 runs for the first time. In later years he made more than 2,000 runs in a season eight times and in 1949 scored 3,429 runs, a seasonal aggregate bettered only by Denis Compton, Bill Edrich and Tom Hayward.

In his first Test, played in 1937 against New Zealand, Hutton made 0 and 1, but in his second he made the first of 19 Test hundreds. He began the 1938 series against Australia with another century and an opening stand of 219 with Charles Barnett. He finished it with his record-breaking 364, made in 13 hours 17 minutes. In the last season before the war he made 196 against the West Indies at Lord's and in the last pre-war Test 73 and 165 not out at The Oval.

The injury to his arm occurred early in the war and subsequently he had three seasons of local and services cricket in which to overcome his disability before first-class cricket began again in 1946.

Many of Hutton's most important innings before the advent of May and Cowdrey were played sustaining an uncertain England batting side. Once at Lord's in 1948 he batted so unimpressively that he was dropped for the next Test – a strange decision in retrospect, for he played Lindwall and Miller at their fastest supremely well. This was especially marked in 1950/1 when he averaged 88.83.

In South Africa in 1948/9 he batted with Washbrook all through a day's play in Johannesburg and they scored 359 for the first wicket. In 1951 he made his 100th hundred at The Oval against Surrey and the next year he captained England against India.

LEP

At Lord's in 1953 he made 145 against Australia and that winter became the first professional to take an MCC side overseas. In the West Indies England lost the first two Tests but won the third and fifth in which the captain made 169 and 205 respectively. Though he missed much of the first series against Pakistan in 1954, his mind was on the tour of Australia where he led England shrewdly and effectively to one of their most decisive victories against the Aussies. His form in the tour matches was as impeccable as ever – he made over 1,000 runs in Australia – but after the two Tests against New Zealand that followed he left international cricket and then announced his retirement from the game after injuries had restricted his appearances for Yorkshire in 1955.

England never lost a Test series under his command – a tribute to his leadership.

After retiring he continued to be involved in the game from the press box and became a Test selector, his deep appreciation of cricket finding a new and most successful outlet.

Ray Illingworth

Born: 8 June 1932, Pudsey, Yorkshire

- He exceeded 1,000 runs in a season eight times, took 100 wickets on ten occasions and completed the double six times.
- He shared the Leicestershire's tenth-wicket stand of 228 with Ken Higgs v Northamptonshire at Grace Road in 1977.
- He took 9 for 42 for Yorkshire v Worcestershre at New Road in 1957 and achieved match figures of 15 for 123 for Yorkshire v Glamorgan at Swansea in 1960.
- He performed the hat trick for Leicestershire v Surrey at The Oval in 1975.
- He achieved the match double (135 runs and 14 for 101) for Yorkshire v Kent at Dover in 1964.

TEST CAREER	
BATTING	
M	61
I	90
NO	11
Runs	1,836
HSc	113
Av	23.23
100	2
50	5
BOWLING	
Runs	3,807
Wkts	122
Av	31.20
Best	6-29
5w	3
10w	–
Ct	45
St	–

RAY ILLINGWORTH played his early cricket for Farsley and by the age of 15 was appearing in their first team in the Bradford League. An innings of 148 not out made over several evenings and attracting a record crowd brought him more than local attention.

Illingworth spent his National Service at RAF Dishforth where he was given plenty of time to further his cricket career with Farsley, Yorkshire Colts, RAF and the Combined Services. He made his Yorkshire

debut in 1951, scoring 56 against Hampshire but still had another year of his National Service to do, so only played in a handful of matches in 1952. However, the following summer he established himself as an important member of the Yorkshire side, scoring his maiden century, 146 not out against Essex at Hull. As a bowler, though, he had to bide his time behind Appleyard and Wardle, and it wasn't until the appointment of Ronnie Burnet as captain that Illingworth came into his own. In 1957 he produced his best bowling figures for the county, taking 9 for 42 against Worcestershire at New Road, and two years later he made his highest score for Yorkshire, hitting 162 against the Indian tourists. He was a member of the team that ended Surrey's domination and gained Yorkshire seven Championships. Then, following a dispute over his contract, he moved to Leicestershire as captain, enjoying a remarkable renaissance that included the captaincy of his country and doubling the length of his international career.

Within months of his move, injury to Colin Cowdrey gave Illingworth the England captaincy. Even after his predecessor was fit, Illingworth remained first choice and

LEP

provided perfect justification for the selectors' decision when his side regained the Ashes in 1970/1 and retained them in 1972. He captained England 31 times and was succeeded by Mike Denness after England were beaten in 1973 by West Indies – Illingworth had chosen to miss the 1972/3 series in India and Pakistan.

Illingworth epitomised the philosophy of the professional. A remarkably shrewd leader, he earned the unyielding respect of his team, although at times his single-mindedness forfeited goodwill. At Sydney in 1970/1 he led his side from the field in protest against some crowd loutishness.

He was a creator of runs rather than a trail-blazer and he would have been even more productive if he had batted higher in the order. He began his bowling career as a medium-pacer before settling into a vein of genuine off-spin with grudging accuracy. By the end of his career he had scored 24,134 first-class runs and taken 2,072 wickets, testimony to his all-round talents. But even more than this, his successful practical brand of captaincy set him apart. With Leicestershire he produced results which must have made every Yorkshire official wince.

Despite the orthodoxy of his own game, he made an enormous impact on the development of cricket, particularly the tactics of one-day competition. He led Leicestershire to wins in the Benson & Hedges Cup in 1972 and 1975 and they were beaten finalists in 1974. That year they also became champions of the John Player League. But Illingworth's greatest triumph in county cricket came in 1975 when he led Leicestershire to their first County Championship.

In 1979 he retired from first-class cricket and returned to Yorkshire as manager. In 1982 in the midst of the troubles which beset the county club, he took over as captain and the following year led Yorkshire to the Sunday League Championship. On leaving Yorkshire for the last time he became a radio and TV commentator before taking up the post of England team manager.

Alan Knott

Born: 9 April 1946, Belvedere, Kent

- His total of 24 dismissals in the 1970/1 series against Australia remained an England record until Jack Russell broke it in 1995/6.
- Against New Zealand in 1970/1 he was dismissed four runs short of becoming the first wicket-keeper to score 100 in each innings of a Test.
- Against Australia at Brisbane in 1974/5 he set a world Test record of 174 catches, beating Godfrey Evans' total. Two years later at The Oval against the West Indies he set the world record of 220 dismissals in his 78th Test.
- He scored 127 not out and 118 not out for Kent v Surrey at Maidstone in 1972.
- He made six dismissals in an innings seven times and nine in a match once for Kent v Leicestershire at Maidstone in 1977.
- His career total of 1,344 dismissals is the fourth highest in first-class cricket and he is one of only twelve to achieve the career double of 10,000 runs and 1,000 dismissals.

AT THE OVAL in 1976 Alan Knott broke the world record for the number of Test victims – a statistic that alone proved the class of the latest in a long line of great wicket-keepers from Kent. A man who always inspired his team-mates with his exuberance and enthusiasm, he also won Test matches with his batting skills.

Knott made his first-class debut for Kent in 1964 and earned his county cap a year later. He was also voted England's Best Young Cricketer of the Year in 1965. In 1967 he arrived on the Test scene with thirteen victims from his two matches against Pakistan. Though still understudy to Jim Parks at the start of the following winter's West Indies tour, he replaced the Sussex wicket-keeper after three drawn Tests. England won the fourth Test on a generous Sobers declaration but only after Knott, with an unbeaten 69, had helped Cowdrey to rectify their first innings. Even more vital was his 73 not out which saved the match and the rubber in the fifth Test.

Now established, his work behind the stumps became an inspiration for every bowler. Neat and lithe, he developed even further agility by continual exercise. His liking for early morning calisthenics earned him a room on his own on more than one tour. On the field his wheeling and stretching between deliveries and battered 'lived-in' pads became trademarks.

An integral part of his county's successes, particularly in one-day cricket, Knott's uninhibited stroke-play brought him five Test centuries. Despite the barrage of short balls in Australia in 1974/5, his 106 not out at Adelaide made him only the second wicket-keeper to reach three figures for England against Australia – his Kent predecessor Les Ames was the other.

It was his batting, too, that showed his character in 1976. After an indifferent start to the series against the West Indies with the bat and behind the stumps, his place became threatened. He responded defiantly by making 116 at Headingley and as England set off for a winter in India and Australia he remained the team's number one wicket-keeper.

It was not until the following spring that his triumphant record-breaking career was threatened. One of the English Packer signatories, he was chosen for the Tests against Australia and continued to justify his inclusion with 12 catches, some of them brilliant. An important 135 in the Trent Bridge Test, his finest Test innings, served to inspire Boycott, who was deeply bogged down in his comeback innings. Knott's strokes were as cheeky and inventive as ever and brought him a five and 18 fours. His final score beat Les Ames's record for a wicket-keeper in England–Australia Tests and the stand with Boycott of 215 equalled the England sixth-wicket record against Australia set in 1939 by Hutton and Hardstaff.

LEP

In 1977/8 he missed the England tour of Pakistan and New Zealand and played instead for Kerry Packer in Australia, thus ending a run of 65 consecutive Tests for his country, a record later equalled by Ian Botham. Returning to England tired after years of continuous cricket, Knott decided not to play for Kent in the following season.

He returned to the Kent side after the establishment made peace with Packer and regained his Test place in 1980. The following year he became the first wicket-keeper to record 100 victims against Australia. But he had expressed an unwillingness to tour regularly which made his Test place insecure and when he joined the South African 'rebels' in 1981/2 he effectively lost it for good. His total of 269 Test victims places him fourth in the list of the world's wicket-keepers but the figure could well have been higher. He retired in 1985.

Jim Laker

Born: 9 February 1922, Frizinghall, Bradford, Yorkshire
Died: 23 April 1986, Putney

- On his Test debut against West Indies in Bridgetown in 1947/8 he took 7 for 103 in his first Test innings, including 6 for 25 on the second morning.
- He set four world records in 'Laker's Match' at Old Trafford in 1956 – most wickets in any first-class match (19); best innings (10 for 53) and match analysis (19 for 90) in Test cricket; first bowler to dismiss all 11 batsmen during a Test.
- In the Ashes series of 1956 he took 46 wickets at 9.60 runs apiece – a record for any series in this country.
- In May 1956 he took 10 for 88 for Surrey v Australians.
- He took 100 wickets in a season 11 times with a best of 166 in 1950.
- He took 8 for 2 for England v The Rest at Bradford in the 1950 Test trial – statistically the most remarkable analysis in English first-class cricket.
- He performed four hat tricks during his career: three for Surrey v Gloucestershire in 1951, v Warwickshire and Cambridge University in 1953; and one for Plum Warner's XI v South of England in 1947.

TEST CAREER

BATTING

M	46
I	63
NO	15
Runs	676
HSc	63
Av	14.08
100	–
50	2

BOWLING

Runs	4,101
Wkts	193
Av	21.24
Best	10-53
5w	9
10w	3
Ct	12
St	–

JIM LAKER will always be remembered for one of the most extraordinary feats in cricket history – his 19 wickets for 90 runs against Australia at Old Trafford in 1956. No one else in the history of the first-class game had ever taken more than 17 wickets in a match. Yet Laker with his off-spin took 19 against Australia while another highly skilled spin bowler, Tony Lock, was taking only one at the other end!

Laker began to bowl off-breaks at the age of 17 having been a batsman and a fast bowler at school. Before Yorkshire could become interested in him, the war broke out. While serving in the RAOC in the Middle East, Laker showed his promise in the good-class cricket played in Cairo. He was stationed in London on his return home and was soon introduced to Surrey who, after a time, convinced him that his future lay in cricket rather than a banking career. No one will ever know whether Yorkshire would have given permission for Surrey to engage Laker had they seen more of his form but in 1946 the memories of his schooldays were over seven years old and they let him go. Within two years of his first-class debut, he was playing for England.

In his first full season, 1947, he finished seventh in the first-class averages with 79 wickets and that winter went to the West Indies with Gubby Allen's MCC team, playing in his first Test in Barbados and taking 7 for 103 in the first innings. Back in England he played in three Tests against Australia, making 63 in a total of 165 in the first.

The Australians of 1948 played him with a confidence their successors seldom emulated. After they had made their 404 for 3 in the last innings at Headingley, Laker, who had had several chances dropped off him but was still really learning the off-spinner's trade, was one of those left out of the side. For a while his career marked time but he burst into the record books in the Test trial at Bradford in 1950 when, on a drying pitch, he took eight 'Rest' wickets for two runs, completely ruining the match as a trial. However, the selectors were still not convinced that he was a valuable bowler on good pitches and he was not a regular choice for England, though his 10 for 119 against South Africa at The Oval in 1951 had much to do with the team's victory there.

In 1952 Surrey's seven-year run of Championship successes began with Laker playing an important part, and in 1953 he and Lock bowled out Australia at The Oval. The Ashes were recovered after 19 years.

Laker's greatest triumphs were to come in 1956 when he took 46 wickets in the series against Australia at an average of 9.60. In addition to his overall bag of 19 wickets at Old Trafford, he became

ES

the first player to take 10 wickets in an innings more than once; he had accomplished the feat earlier in the season with 10 for 88 for Surrey, also against the Australians!

Sadly, his later years with Surrey were marred by disagreements and after his retirement in 1959 he wrote a controversial book which caused the MCC to withdraw his honorary membership and Surrey his pavilion privileges. Happily these were restored within a few years and the incident forgotten. Laker returned to first-class cricket for a time in the early 1960s, playing a number of matches for Essex. When he finally left the first-class scene, he maintained his association with the game, becoming a successful television commentator and writer. He died after a short illness in 1986.

Allan Lamb

Born: 20 June 1954, Langebaanweg, Cape Province, South Africa

- At Old Trafford in the 1984 series against the West Indies he became the first to score hundreds in three successive Tests since Ken Barrington in 1967.
- That summer he equalled the record of four Test hundreds in an English season shared by Herbert Sutcliffe (1929), Don Bradman (1930) and Denis Compton (1947).
- He exceeded 1,000 runs in a season 13 times with a best of 2,049 in 1981.
- He captained Northamptonshire from 1989 to 1995.
- He contributed his highest score of 294 to a South African record fifth-wicket stand of 355 with J.J. Strydom for Orange Free State v Eastern Province at Bloemfontein in 1987/8.

TEST CAREER

BATTING

M	79
I	139
NO	10
Runs	4,656
HSc	142
Av	36.09
100	14
50	18

BOWLING

Runs	23
Wkts	1
Av	23.00
Best	1-6
5w	–
10w	–
Ct	75
St	–

BORN OF ENGLISH parents in a country that was then banished from the cricketing map, Allan Lamb made his England debut almost immediately after becoming qualified by residence in 1982. He had been a regular in the Western Province Currie Cup side in his native South Africa since 1972 and joined Northamptonshire in 1978.

Allan Lamb had a long-standing love affair with Lord's, the headquarters of English cricket. He found the setting inspiring and his record on the ground proved it. His first major match in English cricket

was the Benson & Hedges Final in 1980 in which he played for Northamptonshire against Essex. Lamb's 72 was the decisive contribution to a surprise victory. In the years to come he was to love each return to Lord's.

At the end of the 1984 season he scored 107 in England's first home Test against Sri Lanka but the innings which gave him more pleasure came in late June against the West Indies. It was his century that briefly hinted at a breakthrough in England's fight to shake off the utter dominance of Clive Lloyd's great side. England had taken a first innings lead of 41 thanks to the superb bowling of Ian Botham. Then Lamb set to work, correcting a potential disaster at 33 for 3 and defying Joel Garner and Malcolm Marshall for over six hours. When he was out for 110, England actually declared, whereupon Gordon Greenidge mocked the stiff target of 342. If this was heartbreak for Lamb, there was more agony to follow at the hands of the West Indies. Twice more during that 1984 series he scored battling hundreds for a lost cause. Four years later, he was at it again. Lamb had been out of the England side for some while, his form having lapsed, but England wisely backed his pugnacity against the West Indies and his passion for Lord's. He did not let them down. As England chased an apparently impossible 442 to win a roller-coaster match, Lamb kept the dream alive. No one else in the team managed more than 30 but Lamb battled on to 113 before being run out. He then astounded everyone at Headingley by hobbling out to bat after tearing a calf muscle. He had last been seen on crutches, but he defied the

West Indies pace attack for 87 minutes, batting on one leg and hitting three boundaries. The West Indies bowlers showed him no mercy and despite the pain-killing injection administered just before his journey to the middle, even Lamby frequently winced in agony.

His record in limited-overs internationals is better than his Test history, for he was an outstanding exponent of the game where his powers of improvisation, allied to his fast, aggressive outfielding, assumed great value. After playing a major part in England reaching the 1987 World Cup Final, he was astonishingly omitted from the serious part of the team's convoluted winter.

Returning to the Union, he promptly hit a career-best 294 against a strong Eastern Province side, his 394-minute marathon winning 50,000 rand for sharing a record partnership of 355 and a further 15,000 rand for scoring 150 off fewer than 300 balls and 200 in under 400 balls. It was a fairly strong message to the England selectors.

He became captain of Northamptonshire in 1989, leading them to success in the NatWest trophy in 1992. Although he was a joyful cricketer, a man who lives life to the full, there was considerable criticism of his captaincy and general man-management.

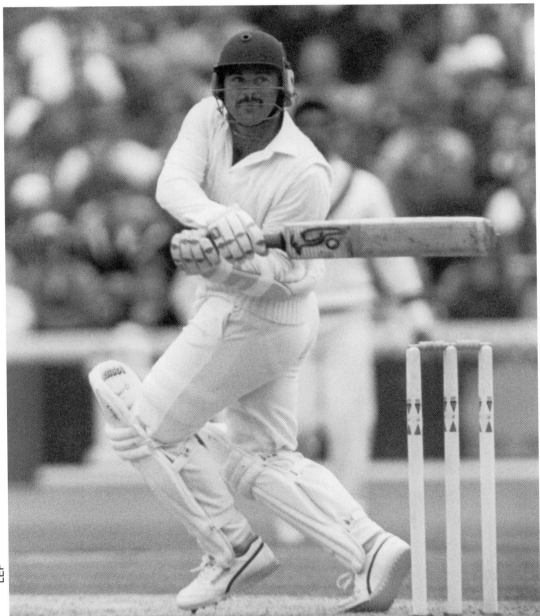

LEP

Tony Lock

Born: 5 July 1929, Limpsfield, Surrey

- He took 100 wickets in a season 14 times, including 200 twice, his 212 wickets at 12.02 apiece in 1957 being the last such instance.
- He took all 10 for 54 for Surrey v Kent at Blackheath in 1956; his analysis of 16 for 83 remains the Surrey record.
- He performed four hat tricks: for Surrey v Somerset in 1955; for MCC in Bahawalpur and Multan in 1955/6; and for Leicestershire v Hampshire in 1967.
- He held eight catches in a match for Surrey v Warwickshire at The Oval in 1957.
- Only Frank Woolley and W.G. Grace have exceeded his first-class career total of 830 catches in the field.
- His career aggregate of 10,342 runs is the highest not to include a century.

TEST CAREER

BATTING

M	49
I	63
NO	9
Runs	742
HSc	89
Av	13.74
100	–
50	3

BOWLING

Runs	4,451
Wkts	174
Av	25.58
Best	7-35
5w	9
10w	3
Ct	59
St	–

TONY LOCK was a remarkable left-arm leg-spin bowler, an extremely useful low-order batsman and a world-class close fielder whose brilliant catching at backward short-leg or off his own bowling has seldom been approached.

Cricket was the abiding passion of Lock's life. At 14 he was playing for Surrey Colts, at 16 in 1946 he joined The Oval staff as a professional and in the same season he played his first county match against Kent. He had to wait almost a year for his next first-class game which was for Surrey against the South Africans. At that time he was purely a 'flight' bowler, his spin almost negligible. When he returned to The Oval in 1949 after two years' National Service, he won a regular team place and took 55 wickets but he realised that his main assets of flight and length were not sufficient. He knew he had to spin the ball enough to disturb good batsmen. For two winters he went to work in the Croydon Indoor School but unhappily for him a low beam in the building made it impossible for him to give the ball any air. However, he was now the ultimate 'killer' as a spin bowler: his break was staggering and his quicker ball came at a wicked pace. His rise coincided with Surrey's. Year after year he swept aside county batsmen with sustained and eager hostility. In 1955 and 1957 he took over 200 wickets and in 1958, only his tenth full season, he reached his 1,500th wicket in first-class cricket.

In 1952 he played his first Test against India at Old Trafford but a few days afterwards, in a county game, he was three times no-balled for throwing and he was 'called' again for illegal delivery on the West Indies tour of 1953/4. The principal cause of the umpires' disapproval seemed to be his faster ball. On MCC's tour of Australia and New Zealand in 1958/9 when the 'throwing' controversy was at its height, Lock was shown a film of himself bowling and he boldly stated that he thought his action unfair. He then decided to revert to his original slow style, concentrating on flight and length, but though his new action was fairly accurate, the old devil was missing.

Omitted from Ted Dexter's tour Down Under in 1962/3, he went there in another capacity – as professional to Western Australia. He spent nine seasons with the team, all but the first as their captain, and led them to the Sheffield Shield title in 1967/8. He also coached the young Dennis Lillee who eventually surpassed Lock's number of wickets for the state. Few bowlers have achieved any success after either changing their action or emigrating. For Lock to do both was extraordinary.

He decided to settle in Perth after retiring from Surrey in 1963 but after just one summer away, he was induced back to county cricket by Leicestershire's secretary, Mike Turner. He was appointed captain in his second season at Grace Road. In 1967, his last season with the county, he led Leicestershire to equal second in the County Championship.

By now, Lock was the most outstanding slow bowler in Australian cricket. Yet even he could have

ES

entertained no thought of an England recall in his 39th year. However, when Fred Titmus was separated from four of his toes in a boating accident, Lock found himself drafted into the Test side in the Caribbean. It was inevitable that he should score 89, his highest Test score, to help England draw the match and therefore win the series.

Devon Malcolm

Born: 22 February 1963, Kingston, Jamaica

- He was named as one of *Wisden*'s Five Cricketers of the Year in 1994.
- His best Test figures of 9 for 57 came against South Africa at The Oval that summer.

TEST CAREER	
BATTING	
M	40
I	58
NO	19
Runs	236
HSc	29
Av	6.05
100	–
50	–
BOWLING	
Runs	4,748
Wkts	128
Av	37.09
Best	9-57
5w	5
10w	2
Ct	7
St	–

THE PATH that took Devon Malcolm from Sheffield United to the England team via Derbyshire CCC wasn't always smooth. In fact, after his first couple of seasons in the Derbyshire side, there were dissenting voices within the club. Some members were not in favour of keeping him.

It was Malcolm's quality of pace that had taken Derbyshire coach Phil Russell into Yorkshire to assess his potential. He had a tip off that Sheffield United had picked up a lad from the Sheffield Works League who was quick and as Derbyshire were desperate for quick bowlers, Russell went to take a look. Malcolm was certainly quick, though he was wild and didn't have much of a run-up.

It was in the summer of 1983 when he was playing for a select Yorkshire League XI against Yorkshire that Malcolm yorked Geoff Boycott and Martyn Moxon in successive overs to inspire the League side to a rare victory over the county. A framed photograph of Boycott's bat coming down just as his middle stump was knocked back takes pride of place in the Malcolm home.

Malcolm made his first-class debut for Derbyshire against Surrey at Chesterfield in 1984. He wasn't really ready for first-class cricket at that stage but because of injuries, the county had no option but to blood him. Though he got plenty of encouragement from the coach and the captain, it was Michael Holding that helped him in all aspects of the game. He made Malcolm realise how important it is to work hard all the time, particularly at the physical side of the game, and to do all the right exercises. Malcolm finally became qualified for England in 1987 and though he was still erratic, his pace inevitably linked him with the Test call-up that eventually came his way at Trent Bridge in August 1989.

It was a measure of Malcolm's improvement that when he made his Test debut he had the best strike rate in the country. He dismissed Australia's Steve Waugh for a duck and might have changed the course of the game had a convincing appeal for leg-before on Geoff Marsh in his opening spell gone his way.

In the Caribbean in 1989/90 the Jamaican-born pace bowler had match figures of 10 for 137, including 6 for 77 in the third Test at Port-of-Spain, Trinidad. In the second innings he dismissed Haynes, Best and Dujon in the space of four deliveries. Pace destroyed all three but when he had to select a ball to make Logie his hat trick victim he picked a bouncer! He won the man-of-the-match award and was the first England bowler since Richard Ellison in 1985 to take ten wickets in a Test match.

A man for the big occasion, Malcolm produced a definitive bowling performance against South Africa at The Oval in 1994. He took 9 for 57 in 16.3 overs to take the sixth-best analysis ever recorded in Test cricket. In three devastating spells he completely destroyed the visitors. His third ball dismissed Gary Kirsten. Then he induced a petrified and inelegant hook from Kirsten's half-brother and ruined Cronje's stumps with a full ball that beat him for pace. Only Cullinan escaped Malcolm's fury before giving Gough his only wicket of the game, but by then Devon had claimed four more scalps. Not once did he bowl a no-ball or a wide as his perfect rhythm homed each delivery on its deadly course. He hit the stumps, hit the 'keeper and first slip, and thudded into pads as South Africa

LEP

crumbled to 175 all out. The crowd was left breathless by Malcolm's brutality and marvelled at the magnificence and unexpectedness of it all.

Though Malcolm's Test career is now at an end, he is still active on the county circuit, playing for Leicestershire after three seasons with Northamptonshire following his departure from Derbyshire.

Peter May

Born: 31 December 1929, Reading, Berkshire
Died: 27 December 1994

- His career best 285 not out is the record Test score at Edgbaston and his stand of 411 with Colin Cowdrey remains England's highest for any wicket.
- He equalled Frank Woolley's England record of 52 consecutive appearances.
- He exceeded 1,000 runs in a season 11 times (plus three on tour), including 2,000 on five occasions.
- He scored five double centuries, including two for Surrey in 1954.
- He twice scored hundreds in three consecutive innings.
- He captained England 41 times with a record 21 wins.

TEST CAREER

BATTING

M	66
I	106
NO	9
Runs	4,537
HSc	285*
Av	46.77
100	13
50	22
Ct	42
St	–

FOR A PERIOD in the 1950s Peter May was regarded as the best batsman in the world. His Test career spanned less than ten years, yet in that time he captained England a then record 41 times.

May was already a batsman of limitless potential when he came under the eye of former England and Leicestershire player George Geary, then coach at Charterhouse. At both Charterhouse and Cambridge May's talents developed on good pitches and he played his first match for Surrey in 1950. A year later he was playing for England against South Africa at Headingley, and it was a sign of the concentration and phlegmatic temperament he was to show so often later that he made 138 in that first Test.

After playing against India in 1952 he became the first target of the Australian bowlers in 1953. Ray Lindwall bowled superbly to him at The Oval in the Surrey match but after he was out cheaply in the first Test the England selectors dropped him until the vital fifth. He returned to play two important innings and was soon acknowledged as the batsman who would take over the mantles of Hutton and Compton.

He was vice-captain to Len Hutton on the triumphant tour of Australia in 1954/5 and it was his 104 at Sydney in the second Test that turned the series towards England after they had lost the first Test and been 74 runs behind in the first innings of the second. On his return to England May found himself appointed captain because Hutton was ill. He led England 35 times in succession, beginning with the magnificent series of 1955 against South Africa. He scored brilliant hundreds at Lord's and Old Trafford, averaging 97.00 in the series.

The following year in a low-scoring series against Australia he averaged 90.00 and shared in a memorable fourth-wicket partnership of 187 with Cyril Washbrook at Headingley after England had lost three wickets for 17 runs.

May was then at his peak and his failure in the Test series in South Africa in 1956/7 has never been satisfactorily explained. He played as well as ever in other matches but fell to brilliant catches and the like in the Tests. But at home in 1957 he soon showed this was merely a fleeting failure, for when England began their second innings in the first Test at Edgbaston 288 behind West Indies, May batted for nearly ten hours, making 285 not out and sharing in a fourth-wicket stand of 411 with Colin Cowdrey.

Early in 1958 May played two of his best innings for Surrey – 174 against Lancashire and Old Trafford and 165 against the New Zealanders at The Oval. But that winter in Australia he led an ageing side and though he still batted well himself, the team were beaten by Richie Benaud's more aggressive Australians. In 1959 May suffered a painful illness midway through the season. He was struck down again during the tour of the West Indies that winter and missed the 1960 season but returned to play against Australia in 1961 before retiring.

LEP

Tall, elegant and powerful, Peter May had an orthodox method. He played very straight and had all the strokes, except perhaps the hook, which he often seemed to need to play. He combined, as few others have, the grace, strength and classic mould of the old-fashioned amateur with the professional competitiveness now needed in the highest class. His services to cricket did not end with his wonderful record on the field. After retiring he served on MCC and TCCB committees and was a Test selector and Chairman of Selectors from 1982 to 1989.

Chris Old

Born: 21 December 1948, Middlesbrough

TEST CAREER	
BATTING	
M	46
I	66
NO	9
Runs	845
HSc	65
Av	14.82
100	–
50	2
BOWLING	
Runs	4,020
Wkts	143
Av	28.11
Best	7-50
5w	4
10w	–
Ct	22
St	–

- In the 1978 Edgbaston Test against Pakistan he took four wickets in five balls to emulate the feat of Maurice Allom.
- He was named a *Wisden* Cricketer of the Year in 1978.
- He scored 100 in 37 minutes for Yorkshire v Warwickshire at Edgbaston in 1977, the third fastest in first-class cricket. It came off 72 balls and his second fifty took just nine minutes.

TALL, STRONGLY built and the brother of an international rugby union player, Chris Old began his career as a hard-hitting left-handed batsman who could bowl, but he ended up succeeding Fred Trueman as Yorkshire's premier new-ball strike force. Occasional matches for Yorkshire from 1966 to 1968 gave the youthful Old little chance to show his pedigree. His first appearance for the county, and his only one of the season, was against Hampshire at Portsmouth in 1966. Yorkshire were impressed by his potential as a fast bowler from the outset but the opportunities were limited until the incomparable Trueman glowered his last for Yorkshire in the summer of 1968. Old's reaction to responsibility and a greatly increased workload was admirable. He topped the Yorkshire averages with 55 wickets at 17.10 runs apiece. Naturally comparisons, odious and otherwise, were initially the order of the day but Old went his own way and in the process proved he was his own man.

Thereafter, his career, nagging injury apart, never really faltered at county level and his potential as a Test player was recognised by selection for a couple of matches against the Rest of the World in 1970 and for the 1972/3 tour of India and Pakistan under the leadership of Tony Lewis. Geoff Arnold's illness let Old in for the second Test and match figures of 6 for 115 and 33 and 17 with the bat, both not out, represented an encouraging start that was developed satisfactorily in India until the slower pitches of Pakistan defeated him.

After that Old was more or less a regular in the England side without quite making the impact his most devoted admirers believed his talent warranted. But then a bone growth in the knee which had been operated on five years earlier brought new trouble in the summer of 1976. He was told that another operation might be advisable but that success could not be guaranteed. Wise advice prevailed, based upon the theory that all other possible cures should be tried first. Treatment at the St James Sporting Clinic, Leeds, brought results bordering on the miraculous.

Old's determination and stamina enabled him to bowl long spells upwind and in hot, steamy climates. His control of line and length was usually outstanding, as when he conceded only 41 runs during 41.40 overs against Pakistan at Headingley in 1978. Earlier in the series at Edgbaston Old had produced his best-ever Test figures, taking 7 for 50 including 4 in 5 balls.

At county level and against anything less than fast-medium, Old was a confident and belligerent striker of the ball, whose driving was high class. But his back-foot defence was awkward and he never learned to cope with short-pitched deliveries. However, in 1977 he made the third fastest first-class century ever – in just 37 minutes against an indifferent Warwickshire attack (his second fifty came in nine minutes).

Old was an enthusiastic, all-purpose fielder and possessed a very safe pair of hands. Appointed captain of Yorkshire in 1981 at the height of the county's internal torment, he was summarily dismissed midway through the following season and made an acrimonious departure for Edgbaston. Sadly, his brief stay there was plagued by an infinite variety of strains and maladies which led to Graham Gooch enlivening the dreary final moments of a Test match with a wicked impersonation of 'Chilly', which involved a dramatic clutching of the back as he was halfway through his run-up.

Geoff Pullar

Born: 1 August 1935, Swinton, Lancashire

- He was the first Lancashire player to score a Test hundred at Old Trafford.
- He took the wicket of West Indies' Frank Worrell with his sixth ball in Test cricket.
- He exceeded 1,000 runs in a season nine times (plus once on tour), including 2,000 twice, notably 2,647 in 1959.
- He was the first Lancashire player to score five hundreds against Yorkshire, including three in 1959.
- He scored seven consecutive first-class fifties in 1959.

TEST CAREER

BATTING

M	28
I	49
NO	4
Runs	1,974
HSc	175
Av	43.86
100	4
50	12

BOWLING

Runs	37
Wkts	1
Av	37.00
Best	1-1
5w	–
10w	–
Ct	2
St	–

ORIGINALLY a middle-order batsman, Geoff Pullar was selected for England as an opener because of his even temperament, very sound defensive technique and left-handedness. The experiment was an instant success: he scored 75 and 131 in his first two outings, formed a lucrative partnership in the Caribbean with another reluctant opener, Colin Cowdrey, and remained an automatic selection for almost four years. Reliable and consistent, his ability to relax and fall asleep instantly and anywhere earned him the unoriginal nickname of 'Noddy'.

He joined Lancashire as an amateur but turned professional in 1956 and after passing 1,000 runs in each of the next two seasons he began the summer of 1959 by playing seven consecutive innings of over 50. That attracted the attention of the Test electors, who had had him on their short list for some time. But their need was for an opening batsman and Pullar had spent his first few seasons at Old Trafford at number 3. He was selected for the third Test at Headingley against India. Ken Taylor and Arthur Milton had opened in the first two matches and Glamorgan's Gilbert Parkhouse returned to partner Pullar after a nine-year absence. Pullar made 75 out of 146, the highest first-wicket partnership for England for 26 Tests.

On 23 July 1959 Geoff Pullar became the first Lancashire cricketer to score a century in a Test at Old Trafford. His innings of 131 was a truly remarkable score and it was extraordinary that he should be the first Lancashire man to break the 100 barrier on home soil considering the earlier prowess of Eddie Paynter, Archie MacLaren, Cyril Washbrook and the Tyldesley brothers.

His sudden rise to eminence earned him the position of England's opening batsman on the 1959/60 winter tour of the Caribbean. The tour showed him to be solid and sound against high pace and bumper attack. He amassed a highly credible 385 runs at an average of 42.77 although his highest score was only 66. He even managed a wicket off the final ball of the last Test match in Trinidad after Peter May, the England captain, had given him the option of the last over of the series – it was the wicket of the venerable Frank Worrell brilliantly caught one-handed at long-off by Fred Trueman.

As England's established opening batsman, he made a career-highest 175 against South Africa at The Oval in the summer of 1960, sharing an opening stand of 290 with Colin Cowdrey by 4 o'clock. He fared badly in two subsequent series against Australia. In the interim he had scored over 1,000 runs on the 1961/2 tour of India and Pakistan, including innings of 119 and 89 in India and 165 in Pakistan. The second of the two series against Australia brought an untimely end to his Test career when he simultaneously strained his groin and tore a cartilage while throwing the ball in.

He had to miss the whole of the 1963 season but after regaining full fitness he returned to the middle-order and spent another five summers at Old Trafford before following David Green to Gloucestershire. The reasons for the likeable Pullar's departure were shrouded in mystery but followed a dressing-down from Lancashire's then chairman, Tommy Higson. He accused Pullar of not trying and being a bad influence. The player refuted these accusations and though Higson resigned, the die had been cast and Pullar was on his way to the West Country. With Pullar opening the batting, Gloucestershire almost landed the County Championship but the discomfort of an arthritic knee persuaded him to remuster as the owner of a thriving sandwich shop.

Author

Derek Randall

Born: 24 February 1951, Retford, Nottinghamshire

- He scored a magnificent 174 in 448 minutes in 1977 as England fell short of the 463 needed to win the Centenary Test in Melbourne.
- His 100 in 406 minutes at Sydney in 1978/9 remains the slowest in England v Australia matches.
- He scored 209 and 146 for Nottinghamshire v Middlesex at Trent Bridge in 1979.
- He was named as a *Wisden* Cricketer of the Year in 1980.
- He exceeded 1,000 runs in a season 13 times with a best of 2,151 in 1985.

DEREK RANDALL gave immense pleasure to spectators and television audiences around the world and emerged as one of the real characters in the game.

For one so dedicated to cricket he came relatively late to the game, making his first-class debut for Nottinghamshire in 1972 at the age of 21. By 1975 he had emerged as one of the best batsmen in county cricket. Facing the Warwickshire attack on a Trent Bridge wicket possessing sufficient pace and bounce to allow Bob Willis to end with match figures of 9 for 106, he hit 153 not out, an innings that included a final fifty in a breathtaking 23 minutes. In 1976 he was chosen for the MCC against the West Indian tourists but two low scores prevented him being picked for a Test match. However, he was brought in for the second of the one-day internationals at Lord's and England were 31 for 4 when Randall went out to the middle. *Wisden* commented: 'England again found consolation in defeat in the performance of one of their young batsmen. This time it was Randall who successfully challenged the West Indies' fast bowlers with a thrilling innings of 88 which included a six and ten fours. He drove their fielders back to the boundary boards in a manner achieved by no other English batsman during the summer. In the third match his innings of 39 off 31 balls brought him the English man-of-the-series award.

That took him to India where he made his Test debut in the second match at Calcutta, scoring 37 as he and Dennis Amiss put on 67 for the third wicket. It proved to be his highest score of the series, though his fielding – a valuable contribution to England's success – kept him in the side for a further 15 consecutive appearances.

The Centenary match in Melbourne was his first Test against Australia and England were set an impossible 463 to win. His splendid innings of 174 took the team to within 45 runs of a much stronger and more confident side. It earned him his Test place in 1977 when England won the Ashes. His innings of 79 at Old Trafford ended unluckily leg-before when Randall was certainly close to his form in the Centenary Test. At Headingley he caught Marsh to give England the rubber and instantly celebrated by turning a rather exuberant cartwheel.

LEP

LEP

Essentially a modest man, he could fidget, fiddle and scratch throughout his innings and his run of ordinary scores on the Pakistan–New Zealand tour of 1977/8 filled him with anxiety. He was chosen for the 1978/9 tour of Australia and every state game brought him a fifty or a century until at Brisbane in the first Test, he made 149 and for once was out. Yet there were many who thought Randall should never have been picked for the tour in the first place. His best innings was a ten-hour 150 at Sydney as England won by 93 runs.

In 1979 he became the only player ever to score a double century (209) and a century (146) in the same match. He did it for Nottinghamshire against Middlesex.

Over the next couple of years Randall played little Test cricket but Nottinghamshire's Championship win in 1981 was a great consolation. Just when it seemed his Test career was over, he was recalled for the first Test of 1982 against India and celebrated with a glorious innings of 126. Touring Australia in 1982/3, he topped the Test averages with 365 runs at 45.63, including a top score of 115 in the first Test at Perth. Following his double failure against the West Indies in 1984 batting in a position to which he had become unaccustomed, his Test career was over.

Randall was an extrovert, effervescent, enthusiastic player. A reporter calling at his home one snowy January was surprised to find Derek casually dressed but wearing a brand new pair of batting pads. 'Just breaking them in for the new season,' he explained. 'Come and meet the missus.' She was sitting in an armchair knitting and wearing another new pair of pads! He communicated a tremendous sense of fun and enjoyment, yet beneath his clowning was a very shrewd cricket brain, a marvellous eye and a gift for improvisation which made him such an exciting player to watch.

Tim Robinson

Born: 21 November 1958, Sutton-in-Ashfield, Nottinghamshire

- Only R.E. Foster has made a higher score in his first Test against Australia than Robinson's 175 in 1985.
- He was a *Wisden* Cricketer of the Year in 1985.
- In January 1988 he hit ten sixes in an innings of 166 for England v Northern Districts at Hamilton, New Zealand.
- He exceeded 1,000 runs in a season 14 times with a best of 2,032 in 1984.
- He captained Nottinghamshire from 1988 to 1995, hitting his highest score of 220 not out against Yorkshire at Trent Bridge in 1990.

TEST CAREER

BATTING

M	29
I	49
NO	5
Runs	1,601
HSc	175
Av	36.38
100	4
50	6
Ct	8
St	–

TIM ROBINSON was a perfectionist. He played very straight, was a patient and watchful batsman, and possessed the very pleasant habit of dispatching off-line balls to the boundary.

At the end of 1984 the Nottinghamshire batsman's most successful season when he scored 2,032 runs at an average of 50.80, he was selected to go on England's tour of India. A great admirer of Geoff Boycott, he soon demonstrated his concentration and phlegmatism. Having made certain of his Test place by scoring 81 in four hours against the Board President's XI at Jaipur, he was unlucky to be given out in each innings of his maiden Test at Bombay. In the first innings he was adjudged caught behind sweeping the leg-spinner when it seemed he was nowhere near it and then in the second innings he was given out leg-before to a ball he may have hit! Yet he left the field both times without a flicker of emotion. He only had to wait a few days until his next Test innings during which he batted for almost ten hours in the heat of Delhi to score 160. His contribution ultimately set England up for victory by eight wickets. There were fears that he might be vulnerable to the leg-before dismissal in India but these were soon quelled, for he adapted himself to the conditions and the front foot quite easily. Robinson was convinced that playing most of his cricket at Trent Bridge, where the wickets in the first half of the 1980s tended to bounce excessively, helped him a lot. It certainly improved his technique and made him a very good back foot player.

In 1985 he was voted one of *Wisden*'s Five Cricketers of the Year. Of his four hundreds at Test level, his 148 against Australia at Edgbaston in 1985 was his lowest. Only R.E. Foster of Worcestershire has made a higher score in his first Test against Australia than Tim Robinson's 175 at Headingley in the 1985 series.

His degree in accountancy and a big interest in the commercial affairs of Nottinghamshire County Cricket Club kept him at home in England during the first few off seasons of his career but he seemed to have established himself as England's opening batsman for many years to come until his visit to the Caribbean in 1985/6. The West Indies' pace attack ruthlessly exploited his technique but not his temperament for Test cricket. In 1987 he bounced back by hitting 166 against Pakistan at Old Trafford. Robinson was quite capable of taking the opposing attack apart and demonstrated this to the full during England's tour of New Zealand in 1987/8. His 166 against the Northern Districts at Hamilton contained a full repertoire of strokes and proved to be a match-winning innings.

His last match for England was the 1988 Test against Sri Lanka at Lord's and his innings was an unbeaten 34. After that, many others were tried in his place and though he scored well for Nottinghamshire, Tim Robinson was continually overlooked. When Nottinghamshire defeated Essex by three wickets in the Benson & Hedges Cup final of 1989, he was at his most fluent and remained in complete control when he was run out 14 short of his century by an over-eager Derek Randall!

It was, of course, Eddie Hemmings who delivered the killer blow in the match but it was Tim Robinson who proudly flourished the Cup and to complete his triumphant day adjudicator Ted Dexter proclaimed him the Gold Award winner.

A great servant of Nottinghamshire County Cricket Club, whom he captained from 1988 to 1995, Tim Robinson played his last game for the county in 1999.

Jack Russell

Born: 15 August 1963, Stroud, Gloucestershire

- He became Gloucestershire's youngest-ever wicket-keeper when he made his debut at 17 years 307 days old against Sri Lanka in 1981.
- During the course of that game, he set a record for most dismissals on a first-class debut (seven catches and a stumping).
- He was named a *Wisden* Cricketer of the Year in 1989.
- He set a new England Test wicket-keeping record in the 1995/6 series against South Africa with 27 dismissals.
- He was made an MBE in 1996.

TEST CAREER	
BATTING	
M	54
I	86
NO	16
Runs	1,897
HSc	128*
Av	27.10
100	2
50	6
Ct	153
St	12

JACK RUSSELL's cricket developed at Stroud CC and at Archway Comprehensive School where he captained, opened the batting and bowled but, like so many gifted sportsmen, never tried his hand at what was to become his natural preserve. On leaving school he trained as an engineer and was studying for an accountancy degree when he gave up both to turn professional with Gloucestershire. He played his first county match at the age of 17 against Sri Lanka, taking seven catches and making a stumping. In 1983, his first full season, he made a great impression, scoring 507 runs and dismissing 63 batsmen (46 caught and 17 stumped) as he emerged as a genuine all-rounder. Awarded his county cap in 1985, he hit his first century for Gloucestershire the following summer when he made 108 against Worcestershire at Hereford in the Sunday League.

On his first overseas tour to Pakistan in 1987/8 when he was the reserve wicket-keeper to Bruce French, Russell played just two days' cricket in eight weeks and so had plenty of time on his hands to pursue his hobby of line drawing. Before he left Britain an art dealer in Bristol had noted his creativity on canvas and had offered to set up an exhibition of Russell's material when he returned. He was swamped by demands for limited editions and commissions for cricketing scenes and portraits.

Russell eventually made his Test debut for England against Sri Lanka in 1988 in what was also his Gloucestershire team-mate David Lawrence's first match. After going in as night-watchman he made 94, the highest individual score of the match. Russell came of age as a Test cricketer against the Australians in 1989, emerging as England's man-of-the-series. At Old Trafford he hit his maiden Test century, an unbeaten 128. His natural brilliance behind the stumps, coupled with a dogged resilience in front of them, stood out among otherwise dispiriting team performances.

As a defensive batsman – number 7 – Jack Russell played a number of innings that saved England from a series defeat. His 55 in the Barbados test of 1989–90 deserves to be ranked

LEP

LEP

alongside any of the country's rearguard actions of recent years, though it was ultimately unsuccessful as Curtley Ambrose took five wickets in as many overs with the second new ball. England, in the shape of Robin Smith and Jack Russell, were inching towards the draw which would have guaranteed them at least the admirable result of a shared series in the Caribbean when Ambrose struck Russell's off-stump so low down that he could have done nothing to protect it. For over five hours he had fought, stepping away after every ball that he survived, banging the ground with his bat and motivating himself verbally to withstand the enemy.

At Johannesburg in November 1995 Russell's partnership with Mike Atherton helped England to draw the game. Monumental defiance was needed and supplied but South Africa were as England had been against New Zealand's Astle and Morrison – conventional!

During the course of his Test career Jack Russell was dropped four times from the England side in mid-series in favour of Alec Stewart – always when England were a Test or two down. Only once did the change work.

One of the most characterful English cricketers, Russell, who has worn the same hat in every first-class match since 1982, drinks anything up to 20 cups of tea a day and actually had a cup of his favourite brew during the drinks interval against Glamorgan at Bristol in 1989.

Mike Smith

Born: 30 June 1933, Westcotes, Leicester

- He exceeded 1,000 runs in a season 19 times (plus once on tour), including 2,000 in six consecutive years (1957–62) and a best season of 3,245 runs in 1959.
- He scored a record July aggregate of 1,209 runs in 1958.
- He is the only batsman to score hundreds in three Varsity matches (201* in 1954, 105 in 1955 and 117 in 1956).
- He holds the Warwickshire records for most runs (2,417 in 1959) and for most catches by a fielder in a career (422), in a season (52 in 1961) and in an innings (6 v Leicestershire at Hinckley in 1962).

ONE OF THE most prolific scorers in post-war cricket, Mike (M.J.K.) Smith was a tall, athletic, middle-order batsman, a superb short-leg fielder and an enormously popular touring captain.

His class was apparent at a young age and some exceptional performances at Stamford earned him his Leicestershire debut during his school holidays. After National Service in the Royal Army Corps, he launched into a brilliant career at Oxford. A Blue all three years and captain in his last, he achieved a triple triumph of a double century and two centuries against Cambridge in the 1950s – his aggregate of 477 runs eclipsed the previous best of 457 by the Nawab of Pataudi in 1929–31.

At first M.J.K. was not intent on pursuing a career in first-class cricket. His early ambition was to gain a foothold as an administrator in the game and so he left Leicestershire to join Warwickshire as assistant-secretary to Leslie Deakins. M.J.K. succeeded Eric Hollies as Warwickshire captain in 1957 and after some good performances was selected to play for England against New Zealand at Edgbaston the following summer. He opened with Peter Richardson and was dismissed for nought in the second over. However, he made ample amends for this reverse when he moved down the order. His maiden century for England against India at Old Trafford in 1959 was followed by 98 (one of three Test dismissals in the nineties) in a record third-wicket stand of 169 with Raman Subba Row against India at The Oval.

In the summer of 1959 M.J.K. hit eight centuries and scored 3,245 runs. He broke the county record held by Norman Kilner and at the beginning of August surpassed the 30-year-old record of Bob Wyatt (2,630) for the most runs scored in a season by a Warwickshire player. At 26 he was the youngest player to reach 3,000 runs, a distinction previously held by Ranjitsinhji. In addition, he demonstrated his prowess as a short-leg fieldsman by breaking Alan Townsend's county record of 42 catches in a season. During the course of 1959 he produced a flurry of sixes in a remarkable match against Gloucestershire. He was unbeaten on 182 as Warwickshire, left to score 318 after being 142 in arrears, won by four wickets.

The demands of cricket prevented M.J.K. from developing his considerable ability as a rugby stand-off half at representative level but he was a member of the Combined Universities side that toured South America in the summer of 1956. Earlier in the year he was selected to play rugby for England, his only Test coming against Wales at Twickenham. But cricket always came first in M.J.K.'s priorities. He continued to play club rugby for Hinckley and occasionally captained Leicestershire, but he did not play a full season after coming down from Oxford.

M.J.K. first took over as England cricket captain on the short tour of India in 1963 but was relieved of the position after England were heavily beaten by the West Indies in the first Test at Old Trafford in

1966. In between times he led his team in 25 Tests. Of his three series as MCC captain abroad, two were drawn in India and Australia; in the other in South Africa, he was the victor.

M.J.K.'s return to first-class cricket with Warwickshire in 1970 after a two-year absence placed him in company with probably the most formidable batting line-up in the county's history. The quintet of Jameson, Amiss, Kanhai, Kallicharran and Smith himself garnered a rich harvest of runs. Warwickshire, a close second to Surrey in the previous year, scored at the rate of 55.75 runs per 100 balls in 1972 in their unbeaten surge to their first Championship for twenty-one years.

M.J.K. Smith, who bridged the traditional and one-day game, later became Warwickshire's chairman.

Robin Smith

Born: 13 September 1963, Durban, South Africa

- He exceeded 1,000 runs in a season 11 times with a best of 1,577 in 1989.
- He was named one of *Wisden*'s Five Cricketers of the Year in 1989.
- He scored an unbeaten 167 against Australia at Edgbaston in 1993, an England one-day international record.
- He became captain of Hampshire in 1998.

A MAJOR FORCE in Hampshire and England cricket, Robin Smith's determination to succeed can be traced back to his early days in South Africa. Robin and his brother Chris grew up in Durban where their father was a very successful saddler to the South African racing industry. So successful, in fact, that he expected his sons to take over the business.

In his final year at school Smith scored six centuries and had an aggregate of 1,780 runs at an average of 85.00, breaking the Natal school records previously held by another distinguished Hampshire old boy, Barry Richards. Smith was only ten when Richards, then with Hampshire, produced a batting book for boys in which all the pictures featured him.

Author

Robin left school a year early because he wanted to make cricket his profession. He wanted to play at Test level and realised that his only real chance lay in England. His decision to qualify for England owed a lot to family persuasion. Brother Chris had moved to the UK when he left school and had a season with Glamorgan's 2nd XI. He enjoyed it so much that when he went home to South Africa he kept telling Robin how great it was to play county cricket for a living.

When Robin left school he came straight to England with Chris, Hampshire acting quickly to offer him a four-year contract after seeing his performances in the nets which fully supported his remarkable record-breaking feats in Natal and South African schools' cricket.

His early sorties into the county game brought him instant success – a Championship debut hundred followed by two more hundreds in the space of ten innings in 1983 were ample proof of his class and temperament. He qualified as an England player at the beginning of the 1985 season, ending the summer with 1,351 Championship runs at 39.73. Known as 'Judge', a nickname given to him because of his wig-like hair, Smith continued to score runs freely and in 1987 recorded his maiden double century – 209 not out against Essex at Southend.

Hampshire supporters found it difficult to understand the prior claims of some of the other young batsmen who were preferred to Smith in the England side but a masterly display of courage, tenacity and technical maturity against a Worcestershire attack consisting of Dilley, Newport and Radford brought him his Test debut. His resolute batting in the last two Tests against the 1988 West Indians provided a much needed source of cheer for English cricket followers in a season of national despair.

He worked hard at his technique during the winter of 1988/9 after the tour of India was cancelled and in 1989 he emerged as England's number one middle-order batsman. His performances in the Ashes series won him a regular Test place and his lone defiance of the Australians brought international prominence – he hit two centuries in a total of 553 runs at 61.44. He ended the summer top of England's Test and Hampshire's batting averages and was the highest-placed English qualified player in the national averages. His decline during the disappointing winter of 1990/1 in Australia was only temporary, for the following summer he scored 416 runs against the West Indies at an average of 83.20.

Smith, a fine one-day player, appeared in 71 limited-overs games for England, scoring an unbeaten 167, an England record, against Australia at Edgbaston in 1993. At Test level his highest score – 175 – came in the fifth Test of the 1993/4 tour of the West Indies at St John's, Antigua. It is hard to believe that Robin Smith, who was appointed captain of Hampshire in 1998, played the last of his 62 Test matches against South Africa in 1995/6, ending with a Test average of 43.67.

John Snow

Born: 13 October 1941, Peopleton, Worcestershire

- He set an England Caribbean series record in 1967/8 when he took 27 wickets at 18.66 runs apiece.
- He took 100 wickets in a season twice
- On the 1967/8 tour of the West Indies he dismissed Gary Sobers first ball at Georgetown for the second time in successive encounters in Tests.
- At The Oval in 1966 he shared a record England v West Indies tenth-wicket stand of 128 with Ken Higgs, both batsmen scoring their maiden first-class fifties. It remains the highest tenth-wicket stand for England at home.

TEST CAREER	
BATTING	
M	49
I	71
NO	14
Runs	772
HSc	73
Av	13.54
100	–
50	2
BOWLING	
Runs	5,387
Wkts	202
Av	26.66
Best	7-40
5w	8
10w	1
Ct	16
St	–

FAST BOWLER John Snow joined Sussex as a batsman but he bowled so quickly and with such movement that anyone who saw him firing away knew he would become a great pace bowler. His progress through first-class cricket was not rapid and he didn't become a regular in the Sussex side until 1964. However, the next season he took over 100 wickets for Sussex and made his Test debut at Lord's against New Zealand in Fred Trueman's last match. Against the West Indies in 1966 Snow took a modest 12 wickets for 37.58 runs apiece, making his most significant contribution at The Oval where he scored 59 in a last-wicket partnership of 128 with Ken Higgs. After a mediocre series against India the following summer he cemented his reputation on England's tour of the Caribbean.

He played in four Tests and took 27 wickets at 18.66, including 7 for 49 on his Caribbean debut at Kingston and 5 for 86 in the next Test at Bridgetown. In the fifth Test at Georgetown he dismissed Gary Sobers first ball, just as he had done at The Oval in 1966, to finish with ten wickets in the match including 6 for 60.

Once again supported by David Brown, Snow took 17 wickets against the Australians in 1968 but his best series came on the controversial Ashes tour of Australia in 1970/1. In six Tests Snow took 31 wickets at 22.83 runs apiece, finishing off the fourth at Sydney with his best Test figures of 7 for 40. Graham McKenzie, playing in his last Test, had to leave the field with blood streaming from his face after being hit by a Snow delivery that climbed after pitching on a good length. Snow's shock bouncer was a difficult weapon to counter at any time, but when he bowled it around the wicket it became almost impossible to fend off.

In the seventh Test, again at Sydney, England needed a draw to win the Ashes. Umpire Lou Rowan cautioned Snow for intimidatory bowling and the pair clashed. When Snow went off to field at long leg, in front of the notorious Paddington Hill, a drunken spectator reached over the fence to grapple with him and the fast bowler was showered with beer cans. Illingworth led his team from the field and the umpires warned the Englishmen that the game would be forfeited and the Ashes also. In the second innings

LEP

LEP

Australia needed only 223 to win, but even with Snow in hospital, after breaking the index finger of his bowling hand, England won by 62 runs.

The England pace bowler was embroiled in controversy again during the summer of 1968. In the first test at Lord's Snow scored 73, his highest knock at international level. It was in this match that he knocked Gavaskar off his feet as the Indian was trying for a quick single. Snow was ordered to apologise and he was left out of the team for the Old Trafford Test as a punishment.

Sadly, he never toured again with England and he gained a reputation for being moody and obstinate. However, he was England's answer to Dennis Lillee and Bob Massie during the 1972 campaign against Australia, taking 24 wickets at 23.12 runs apiece and helping his side to draw the series 2–2 to retain the Ashes he had won for them some 18 months earlier.

He might well have been the first to challenge Fred Trueman's record of 307 Test wickets but for injury and the intervention of Kerry Packer. Snow, who took 883 wickets for Sussex, is likely to remain the only international fast bowler to have two volumes of verse published.

Brian Statham

Born: 17 June 1930, Gorton, Manchester

- Against South Africa at Lord's in 1960 he produced the first ten-wicket analysis by an England fast bowler in post-war Tests.
- He exceeded 100 wickets in a season 13 times.
- He holds the Lancashire career record for most wickets with 1,816.
- He performed the hat trick on three occasions: for Lancashire v Sussex at Old Trafford in 1956 and v Leicestershire at Old Trafford in 1958, and for MCC v Transvaal at Johannesburg in 1956/7.

DURING A CAREER lasting 19 years Brian Statham was a highly popular player both on and off the field; everyone admired the level-headed manner in which he dealt with adversity as well as adulation. Most fast bowlers possess a volatile nature that sometimes gets them into trouble but there was never the slightest suggestion of Statham giving offence. In this way he contrasted markedly with his England partner Fred Trueman: the Yorkshireman was all fire and brimstone, the Lancastrian more phlegmatic.

After National Service in the RAF, Statham joined Stockport in the Central Lancashire League. He did nothing exceptional there, but his potential was recognised and MCC suggested that he contact his county club, who offered him a trial. Taken on in May 1950, he came under the guidance of Harry Makepeace and made such rapid progress that within two months he was making his Championship debut against Kent at Old Trafford on his 20th birthday. A few weeks later he gained a regular place in the county side. Though he was somewhat raw and his action looked ungainly, there was no denying that he possessed speed and he had several successes, notably at Bath where in one spell he took five Somerset wickets for five runs. His remarkably quick advance was far from over and before the summer ended he had been awarded his county cap. That winter, together with his team-mate Roy Tattersall, he was called upon to reinforce the injury-hit MCC team in Australia. He did not play in any Tests there but made his England debut against New Zealand at Christchurch.

Lancashire were obviously delighted with his progress and in his second season he made his mark with 97 wickets at 15.11 apiece. Known for a time as 'The Whippet', he gradually filled out and developed powerful shoulders which gave him added pace. From the time he made his Test debut Brian Statham was usually an automatic choice for England, featuring in the strong sides that won and retained the Ashes in the 1950s. His partnerships with Frank Tyson and Fred Trueman often found him playing a supporting role but neither would deny the large part he played in their own successes. However, with just a little bit more luck he could have been the more successful partner.

After 1963 it seemed that Statham's Test career was over but he came back for one match against South Africa at The Oval in 1965 and with 5 for 40 and 2 for 105 completed 250 test wickets. Among them were his 7 for 39 against South Africa at Lord's in 1955 and 7 for 87 against Australia at Melbourne in 1958/9.

Outside Test cricket he topped 100 wickets in 13 seasons, ten in succession from 1957 to 1966, and his triumphs included three hat tricks: against Sussex at Old Trafford in 1956, for MCC against Transvaal at Johannesburg in 1956/7 and against Leicestershire, again at old Trafford, in 1958. At Coventry in 1957 he took 15 wickets (8 for 34 and 7 for 55) in the match with Warwickshire and another 15 (7 for 71 and 8 for 37) against Leicestershire in 1964.

MEN

Statham's benefit in 1961 showed the esteem in which he was held for it brought him over £13,000. In 1965 he took over the captaincy of Lancashire and in the New Year's Honours List of 1966 he was made a CBE. The next season, however, he relinquished the county leadership. He retired in 1968.

Few bowlers have attained such accuracy at such a biting pace but Statham had his own dictum and his own motivation: 'If they miss, I hit,' he would explain with a wry smile.

David Steele

Born: 29 September 1941, Bradeley, Staffordshire

- He exceeded 1,000 runs in a season ten times.
- He dismissed Australia's Ashley Mallett with his fourth ball in Test cricket.
- He performed the hat trick for Derbyshire v Glamorgan at Derby in 1980.
- He achieved the match double (130 runs and 11 wickets) for Northamptonshire v Derbyshire at Northampton in 1978.
- He holds the Northamptonshire career record for most catches by a non-wicket-keeper with 469.

TEST CAREER	
BATTING	
M	8
I	16
NO	0
Runs	673
HSc	106
Av	42.06
100	1
50	5
BOWLING	
Runs	39
Wkts	2
Av	19.50
Best	1-1
5w	–
10w	–
Ct	7
St	–

DAVID STEELE was England's folk hero of the mid-'70s. Called up for Test duty against Australia in his 35th year, the bespectacled and prematurely grey batsman looked remarkably like a Home Guard character from *Dad's Army*!

It was in the cramped backyard of an unpretentious semi in the suburbs of Stoke-on-Trent that the young Steele, in company with his mentor Uncle Stan Crump and cousin Brian (also of Northamptonshire and a fine prospect until the mantle of stock bowler fell on him), learned the basic skills of batting and bowling. They played outside in the off season for the simple reason that there were no local indoor schools at the time. In the summer Uncle Stan extended the experience of the two boys by running a Sunday side.

Author

When he reached 18 Steele joined Crump in the Sneyd Colliery side. The following year he was appointed professional at Hartshill and his performances over the next couple of years led to an offer to join Derbyshire. However, he preferred to link up with his cousin Brian and Northamptonshire. As a league player he had been expected to both bat and bowl and though he took 8 for 29 against Leicestershire in 1966 with his leg-breaks, he wisely decided to concentrate on his batting.

Though Northamptonshire were well served by batsmen Brian Reynolds, Colin Milburn, Roger Prideaux and Hylton Ackerman, these players were soon lost to the club and by 1972 the county had the appearance of an unbalanced side. Steele and Pakistani star Mushtaq Mohammed took the batting load and Steele with 1,618 runs at an average of 52.19 had his best-ever season.

He must have thought he would never be recognised by England but in 1975 when the selectors turned to him in an hour of desperate need, he was still eager for the challenge. Preparing for his twelfth full season – different only because it was his benefit year – the World Cup and the four Ashes Tests seemed outside his orbit and strictly reserved for the glamour boys. Yet by the end of the year he

LEP

was BBC Sports Personality of 1975, *Daily Express* Sportsman of the Year, BBC *Grandstand* Sportsman of the Year, etc, etc. He was also £25,000 better off after a record benefit for Northamptonshire and was a world-famous player with enough status to turn down the county captaincy in order to concentrate on his batting.

Once he had found his way to the middle (he miscalculated the stairs and found himself in the gents en route to his first Test innings) he produced a succession of staunch displays against Lillee, Thomson and Walker, who were all in their prime. Limitless courage, tenacity and concentration, plus a sound defence and a fine array of attacking strokes, brought him 365 runs and four fifties in his first three Tests. It later emerged that Steele had struck a bet with his local butcher who duly stocked the player's freezer with 365 lamb chops and four fillet steaks.

He produced similar heroics against the 1976 West Indians, scoring his maiden Test century in the drawn game at Trent Bridge, and was desperately unlucky to be omitted from England's subsequent tour of India because of doubts about his technique against spin. In 1979 Steele moved to Derbyshire after being offered the captaincy but he resigned the office after only two months and returned to Northamptonshire at the end of his three-year contract.

Steele by name and steel by nature, he was a dedicated and worthy player who did much to restore England's shattered pride and hope in the unforgettable summer of 1975.

Alec Stewart

Born: 8 April 1963, Merton, Surrey

TEST CAREER	
BATTING	
M	115
I	207
NO	17
Runs	7,469
HSc	190
Av	39.31
100	14
50	38
BOWLING	
Runs	13
Wkts	0
Av	–
Best	–
5w	–
10w	–
Ct	220
St	11

- He was named as a *Wisden* Cricketer of the Year in 1992.
- He has appeared in 137 limited-overs internationals – an England record.
- He has exceeded 1,000 runs in a season eight times with a best of 1,665 in 1986 and a highest score of 271 not out v Yorkshire at The Oval in 1997.
- He was made an MBE in 1998.
- He equalled the world record of 11 catches in a match v Leicestershire at Grace Road in 1989.

THE RISE OF model professional Alec Stewart to the position of England captain surprised many. It wasn't that the pedigree was absent, for his family environment was conducive to the production of a young sportsman – his father Mickey, a former Test player and Surrey captain, also managed England and his mother Sheila was a top netball and hockey player. But even though Stewart was a good batsman and wicket-keeper, he was considered low down in the pecking order for the England captaincy.

On joining Surrey Stewart simultaneously began an association with Australian grade cricket, playing season after season with the Midland Guildford club in Perth.

If his batting skills were learned at The Oval, then it was the Aussie school of hard knocks that instilled in him a mental toughness, a desire to give as good as he got.

Success certainly didn't come easily to Alec Stewart. Though he has always appeared to be a well-organised, busy, bat-twirling player, capable of making entertaining runs, in the early days he seemed to lack the commitment needed to register big scores. In fact, if Stewart hadn't developed his wicket-keeping, he may not have received his chance in international cricket as early as he did.

Stewart made his first-class debut for Surrey against Gloucestershire in 1981. It was his only first-team appearance of the summer. Again in 1982 he played just one game but in 1983 he established himself in the Surrey side, scoring his maiden first-class century, 118 not out against Oxford University. He continued to score runs freely and in 1986 topped the county batting averages with 1,665 runs at 46.54. His total included three centuries and a highest score of 166 against Kent at The Oval. Stewart topped the Surrey batting averages again the following summer and after a successful 1989 season when his 1,633 runs at 45.36 included his first double hundred – 206 not out against Essex – he was selected to tour the West Indies, making his Test debut in a nine-wicket win at Sabina Park, Kingston. Also during the course of

LEP

1989 Stewart, who had replaced Jack Richards as Surrey's wicket-keeper, held 11 catches in the match against Leicestershire at Grace Road, thus equalling the world first-class record.

At Test level Stewart was dropped after the disastrous tour of Australia in 1990/1 but was recalled – much to everyone's surprise – to keep wicket in the final Test against the West Indies in the summer of 1991. It was an opportunity he could not afford to miss and he took it. England won by five wickets. Two weeks later he scored his first Test century, 113 not out against Sri Lanka at Lord's. Stewart's highest Test score of 190 was made against Pakistan at Edgbaston in 1992 and he ended the series as England's leading run-getter with 397 runs at 56.71.

Captain of England on 14 occasions, the highlight of his spell in charge was the home series triumph over South Africa in the summer of 1998. He went on to skipper England during the World Cup of 1999 when the home side were very disappointing. He was the leading run-maker in Test cricket during the 1990s, scoring 6,407 runs at an average of more than 40. He narrowly pipped Mark Waugh to this honour while making 95 against South Africa at Durban in December 1999. In the summer of 2000 he overtook Graham Gooch as England's most capped one-day player and has appeared in 137 matches at the time of writing. Also during that summer he equalled Adam Gilchrist's one-day record for most wicket-keeping dismissals – six against Zimbabwe at Old Trafford.

Though he decided to miss the visits to India and New Zealand in the winter of 2001/2, his massive contribution to English cricket over the past decade cannot be over-estimated.

LEP

Bob Taylor

Born: 17 July 1941, Stoke-on-Trent, Staffordshire

- He was the first England wicket-keeper to catch five Australian batsmen in an innings in the Brisbane Test of 1978/9.
- In the Test against India at Bombay in 1979 he set a world record with ten catches in the match. His seven catches in the first innings equalled Wasim Bari's world record.
- Against Australia at Headingley in 1981 he exceeded John Murray's world record of 1,270 first-class catches.
- He holds world records for most wicket-keeping dismissals and catches in a first-class career with 1,649 (1,473 caught and 176 stumped).
- He holds the Derbyshire career record for most dismissals – 1,304.
- He made ten dismissals for Derbyshire in the match against Hampshire at Chesterfield in 1963.
- He made seven dismissals in an innings for Derbyshire on two occasions: v Glamorgan at Derby in 1966 and v Yorkshire at Chesterfield in 1975.

TEST CAREER

BATTING

M	57
I	83
NO	12
Runs	1,156
HSc	97
Av	16.28
100	–
50	3

BOWLING

Runs	6
Wkts	0
Av	–
Best	–
5w	–
10w	–
Ct	167
St	7

IF EVER A ROLE model were required for the ideal sportsman, the complete professional, it would be hard to think of anyone to challenge Derbyshire's wicket-keeper Bob Taylor.

He graduated to the Derbyshire team via Staffordshire, replacing George Dawkes who needed a cartilage operation then hurt his knee again in a car accident and decided to retire. Like many a 'keeper before him Taylor liked to be regarded as a bit of a batsman but it was batting that nearly cost him his left eye. On a turning wicket at Grace Road he attempted to sweep Jack Birkenshaw but the ball was a

quicker one, lifted off the end of his bat and struck him in the eye. For three weeks he was lying on his back with a detached retina and haemorrhaging, wondering whether he would play again and it was with some trepidation that he later faced Harold Rhodes in the indoor nets.

When he played in his first Test match at Christchurch, New Zealand, in 1971 he had already been on one MCC tour – to the Far East in 1969/70 when no Test matches were played. In 1971/2 he toured Australia with the so-called World XI and the following winter he should have gone to India and Pakistan with MCC but an ear infection kept him at home at the last minute.

For the next six years Taylor was condemned to the role of understudy to Alan Knott on winter tours. For a while there was little to choose between their keeping, the Kent player's brilliant batting gaining preference. After that he was more fortunate, mainly as a result of the big money put up by Kerry Packer, which left the way open for Taylor to establish himself as England wicket-keeper. His successes behind the stumps spanning the years 1977 to 1984 prove how incredibly lucky

LEP

England were to have in reserve a craftsman of such a high standard. He also showed he was no slouch with the bat, scoring 97 in the fifth Test at Adelaide in January 1979. On that occasion he shared in a match-winning seventh-wicket stand of 135 with Geoff Miller which was only eight runs short of the record. After equalling that score while playing for the International Wanderers against a South African Invitation XI in Johannesburg he eventually reached his maiden century for Derbyshire against Yorkshire in 1981.

Against India in Bombay in the Golden Jubilee Test, Taylor caught seven batsmen in India's first innings to equal Wasim Bari's 1978/9 Test record at Auckland and then went on to create a new world record – ten victims in a Test match – when he caught three more in the second innings. Moreover, when he came out to join Botham England were in deep trouble at 58 for 5. Bob scored an invaluable 43 and helped his captain add 171 for the sixth wicket – a new record for England v India. The match was won by ten wickets.

As a wicket-keeper Bob Taylor was a perfectionist and maintained a consistency of form and fitness second to none. He once dropped Roy Fredericks three times in quick succession standing up to Ian Buxton, though perhaps only he would have classed them as chances. By the same token, he missed so little standing back that Alan Ward once checked with an opposing batsman that he really had got a touch before accepting that Taylor had actually dropped a catch off him.

Taylor was his own severest critic and the spectator could often tell whether a chance had escaped by watching to see if his head went down for a few moments before the next delivery. By the time of his retirement in 1984 Bob Taylor had shared in the dismissal of 1,304 batsmen for Derbyshire and 1,649 in all matches – a world record.

Graham Thorpe

Born: 1 August 1969, Farnham, Surrey

- He scored 114 not out against Australia at Trent Bridge on his Test debut in 1993.
- He has exceeded 1,000 runs in a season eight times with a best of 1,895 runs in 1992.
- He was named as a *Wisden* Cricketer of the Year in 1997.
- He scored 223 not out for an England XI against South Australia at Adelaide in 1998/9.

TEST CAREER

BATTING

M	73
I	134
NO	18
Runs	4,857
HSc	200*
Av	41.87
100	10
50	29

BOWLING

Runs	37
Wkts	0
Av	–
Best	–
5w	–
10w	–
Ct	81
St	–

ONE OF THE WORLD'S best left-handed batsmen, Graham Thorpe is a Surrey boy, born and bred in Farnham and still living there now.

From a very young age it was possible to detect in him the attributes that were necessary to transport his obvious talent on to the international stage. Most striking was his temperament, which enabled him to adapt quickly and to flourish at every level at which he has played the game. He has never been out of his depth. At school he was as good at football as he was at cricket and played in midfield for England Schoolboys. Brentford showed an interest but cricket was his first love and by the age of 15 he was scoring centuries for Farnham 1st XI. A year later he became an automatic choice for Surrey Under-19s. As soon as he joined the playing staff at The Oval in 1988 he was earmarked as a first-class cricketer, although he forced his way into the first team primarily as a bowler who batted.

In 1989 at the age of 19 he hit a brave century against a Hampshire side including West Indian pace bowler Malcolm Marshall. He ended his first season with 1,132 runs at an average of 45.28. His reward for an immensely promising full debut season was a place on the England 'A' tour of Zimbabwe, an expedition which convinced most judges that a full England cap was only another good season away. Though he continued to score runs freely for the next few seasons (including 1,895 at 45.58 in 1992), it was the summer of 1993 before he finally made the senior side.

Making his England debut against Australia in the third Test at Trent Bridge, Thorpe scored an unbeaten 114 in his country's second innings in a drawn game. This was story book stuff but the story does have a twist – the previous two Englishmen to do this, Jackie Hampshire and Frank Hayes, never managed it again. Thorpe had to wait until his 15th Test appearance for his second century, 123 against Australia at Perth in 1994/5.

The following summer Thorpe failed to register a century in the series against the West Indies – his highest score being an innings of 94 at Old Trafford – but he was England's leading run-getter with 506 at an average of 42.16. Thorpe's highest score at Test level came against Australia at Edgbaston in 1997 when his innings of 138, coupled with Hussain's 207 in a fourth-wicket partnership of 288, helped England to win by nine wickets. Thorpe ended the series as England's top batsman with 453 runs at an average of 50.33.

Thorpe risked his Test future by not making himself available for England's tour to South Africa in 1999/2000, putting his family first. England certainly missed him. However, he was rightfully restored to the line-up against Zimbabwe and West Indies the following summer. He was a major success for England on the winter tours of Pakistan and Sri Lanka. He scored his seventh Test century, 118 against Pakistan in Lahore, in November 2000 when he shared in a 166-run partnership with Craig White. Just as important was his unbeaten 64 in fading light in Karachi where England secured their first Test series win in Pakistan for 39 years.

After a brief rest at home he flew to Sri Lanka for the second stage of England's winter tour. More solid batting from Thorpe helped the team secure their fourth successive series win, scoring 269

LEP

runs at 67.25 against the magic of Muttiah Muralitharan. He batted for a total of six and a half hours in the crucial third Test at Colombo, remaining undefeated with match-winning knocks of 113 and 32. During the course of the tour to New Zealand in 2001/2 Thorpe hit his highest ever Test score of 200 not out in the first Test at Christchurch, a match which England won by 98 runs.

Thorpe – an unusual mixture of brilliance and resilience – has all the qualities that the England fans love to see – grit, flair and guts.

Fred Titmus

Born: 24 November 1932, St Pancras, London

- He took four wickets for five runs in 58 balls on the second day of the Sydney Test against Australia in 1962/3.
- He exceeded 1,000 runs in a season eight times and took 100 wickets 16 times, notably 191 in 1955. He completed the double eight times.
- He holds Middlesex career records for the most appearances (642), most wickets (2,361) and most instances of 100 wickets in a season (11).
- He twice took nine wickets in an innings for Middlesex: 9 for 52 v Cambridge University at Fenner's in 1962 and 9 for 57 v Lancashire at Lord's in 1964.
- He returned a match analysis of 15 for 95 for Middlesex v Somerset at Bath in 1955.
- He performed the hat trick for Middlesex v Somerset at Weston-super-Mare in 1966.

TEST CAREER

BATTING

M	53
I	76
NO	11
Runs	1,449
HSc	84*
Av	22.29
100	–
50	10

BOWLING

Runs	4,931
Wkts	153
Av	32.22
Best	7-79
5w	7
10w	–
Ct	35
St	–

FRED TITMUS'S promotion from ground staff to the Middlesex 1st XI had a story book touch about it. It happened in June 1949 when Middlesex, with Robertson, Compton, Edrich, Mann and Young engaged in the first Test match against New Zealand at Lord's, found themselves short for their game against Somerset at Bath. Walter Robbins and Gubby Allen went out to the nets to have a look at the aspiring talent being coached by Fowler and Watkins and collected Titmus. So instead of selling scorecards at the Test, he was in the Middlesex side, aged 16 years and six months.

His career was subsequently interrupted by National Service in the Royal Air Force but he got in plenty of cricket for the RAF and Combined Services; his first trip in an aeroplane piloted by future Nottinghamshire secretary Bob Wilson was to play cricket for Combined Services.

LEP

The summer of 1955 saw Titmus, aged 22, establish himself among the leading all-rounders by recording his first double in remarkable fashion. His total of wickets bounded to 191 for an average of 16.31 and he nearly doubled his runs by scoring 1,235 with a highest of 104. His tally of 158 wickets in all matches for Middlesex beat the previous county record set up by Albert Trott with 154 back in 1900. In 1959 and the three following seasons Titmus did the double in Championship matches alone, going on to do it on a total of eight occasions and taking 100 wickets 16 times in all. In 1962 he produced the best bowling figures of his career when he took 9 for 52 against Cambridge University at Fenner's. This led to his being chosen for the 1962/3 tour of Australia and New Zealand where he was one of three off-spinners – a selection pretty strongly criticised on the grounds of imbalance. The three were Allen, Illingworth and Titmus with Titmus not expected to be the front-runner. As events turned out, he was. At Sydney he took 7 for 79, including the wickets of Simpson, Harvey, Booth and O'Neill. He took 21 wickets in the Tests (one more than Fred Trueman achieved), had a batting average of 36.40 and was bracketed with Ken Barrington

as the outstanding success of the tour. Titmus established himself as an international player and at Headingley in 1965 he took four wickets in six balls against New Zealand as England ran out winners by an innings and 187 runs.

Having played in the first two Tests in the West Indies in 1967/8, Fred Titmus was involved in a boating accident in Barbados in which he lost four toes on his left foot. He returned home with his future as a cricketer in serious doubt. Ray Illingworth moved into the England side and proved successful. Despite Titmus's remarkable recovery, the place was never there for him again but in 1968, playing in a specially fitted boot, he took 100 wickets and scored 924 runs, narrowly missing another double.

In 1974 at the age of 42 he was sent to Australia with Mike Denness's side and was able to weather some of the hostile bowling by Lillee and Thomson, scoring a gutsy 61 on a fast Perth pitch. He retired in 1976 to coach at The Oval. There he made one first-class appearance for Surrey before returning to his Hertfordshire sub-post office. He was persuaded to play a number of further games for Middlesex, his last in 1982 by which time Titmus had played for the county in five decades. One of only five cricketers to have scored over 20,000 runs and taken 2,500 wickets, he was a Test selector for three seasons.

Fred Trueman

Born: 6 February 1931, Stainton, Yorkshire

- On his Test debut against India at Headingley in 1952 he reduced India to 0 for 4 in their second innings by taking three wickets in eight balls.
- That same series he achieved a record England v India innings analysis of 8 for 31 and set a series record with 29 wickets.
- Against Australia at Headingley in 1961 he took 5 for 0 with 24 off-cutters at a reduced pace.
- In 1963 he set an England v West Indies series record with 34 wickets and at Edgbaston had match figures of 12 for 119, ending with a 6 for 4 spell from 24 balls.
- He was the first bowler to take 300 wickets in Test cricket.
- He took 100 wickets in a season 12 times, with a best of 175 in 1960.
- He performed the hat trick on four occasions, three of them for Yorkshire against Nottinghamshire – at Trent Bridge in 1951, at Scarborough in 1955 and at Bradford in 1963. His other hat trick came in a match against MCC at Lord's in 1958.

TEST CAREER	
BATTING	
M	67
I	85
NO	14
Runs	981
HSc	39*
Av	13.81
100	–
50	–
BOWLING	
Runs	6,625
Wkts	307
Av	21.57
Best	8-31
5w	17
10w	3
Ct	64
St	–

CHARACTERS IN CRICKET are not appreciated until they have retired or at least reached a seniority that gives their peculiar individuality a lovable quality. Thus it was some time before Fred Trueman, 'Fiery Fred' to many, was fully appreciated in all quarters.

The son of a miner, Trueman worked briefly in the pits before making his first appearance for Yorkshire at the age of 18. His immense promise was obvious but he was brought along gradually during the next few years, two of which were spent doing National Service in the RAF. He was in some ways lucky to play in his first Test in 1952 against Indian batsmen on lively pitches and in four Tests he took 29 wickets at 13.31 apiece, including 8 for 31 at Old Trafford. The next year, however, he played only once against Australia. That winter he went to the West Indies with Len Hutton's team but in the turbulent atmosphere of cricket there, his brash forthright manner frequently had him in trouble. Though he took 134 wickets at home in 1954 the selectors did not call on him for Australia. The Ashes were won without him. He was not fit in 1956 and was again left out of a touring side, this time to South Africa.

By this stage in his career he had gained experience and from about 1957 to 1963 he was at his peak. In 1960 he had his best home season, taking 175 wickets, and it was not until 1967 that he again took fewer than 100. In all he took 100 wickets in a season 12 times and among bowlers of similar pace only Brian Statham has achieved the figure more often. In his later years a touch of prudence made his batting more productive overall and his three first-class hundreds were made between 1963 and 1965.

Valuable though he was to Yorkshire, it was in Test matches that the real class of his bowling was shown by his ability to surprise the world's leading players. In 1960 in the West Indies he took 21 Test wickets and kept clear of the controversy that had surrounded him on the previous tour. At home that year he took 25 wickets against South Africa and in 1961 20 more against Australia, including 5 for 58 and 6 for 30 at Headingley where he made the most of a poor wicket and enabled England to win by eight wickets. At Lord's in 1962 he took 6 for 31 when Pakistan were bowled out for 100 on the first day and in the series he added 22 wickets to the growing list. Against Frank Worrell's triumphant West Indians of 1963 he took 11 wickets in the famous Lord's Test, followed by 12 at Edgbaston. His 7 for 44 in the last innings then brought England their only win and was a model of how conditions that allowed the ball to move in the air and off the seam could be exploited. In that series his tally of wickets was 34: the next most successful English bowler's haul was 18. In the 1964 series against Australia he was still the major wicket-taker but was dropped for the fourth Test and there were suggestions that his

LEP

Test career might be over. However, he was recalled for the final test at The Oval, where he dismissed Redpath and McKenzie with successive balls before shortly afterwards making Neil Hawke his 300th victim amid universal jubilation.

His farewell season might almost have been stage-managed. Yorkshire won their third successive Championship and with Trueman at the helm inflicted the first defeat on the 1968 Australians. Trueman was Yorkshire to the core which made incongruous a brief return in one-day matches for Derbyshire. He joined BBC Radio's *Test Match Special* team where his comments earned less respect than his bowling had!

Frank Tyson

Born: 6 June 1930, Farnworth, Bolton, Lancashire

- He took 101 wickets in 1957.
- He took 6 for 16 in 51 balls as Australia's last eight wickets fell for 34 runs in the Melbourne Test of 1954/5.
- His best bowling figures were 8 for 60 (13 for 112 in the match) against Surrey at The Oval in 1957.

TEST CAREER	
BATTING	
M	17
I	24
NO	3
Runs	230
HSc	37*
Av	10.95
100	–
50	–
BOWLING	
Runs	1,411
Wkts	76
Av	18.56
Best	7-27
5w	4
10w	1
Ct	4
St	–

'TYPHOON' was an apt nickname for Frank Tyson, for he caused havoc at his peak but then blew himself out, as was to be expected from an extremely physically strong bowler relying on excessive pace without swing or subtleties.

Pawing the ground like an angry bull as he started his run, Tyson sent gasps of astonishment around the ground. His swift run was somewhat ungainly and was followed by a wide-arm swing and a strong body action to generate pace.

He was destined for big things right from his very first delivery in county cricket, playing for Northamptonshire under the guidance of Freddie Brown in 1952. He came along at a period when Fred Trueman and Brian Statham were already established in the England side. Though such glorious fast bowlers surrounded him, he is probably remembered as one of the most terrifying quick bowlers England has ever produced, Harold Larwood being the other.

Against the Australian tourists in 1953 he was bowling express pace, but no one expected the carnage of the following Ashes series in Australia. Tyson had made his England debut in the fourth Test at The Oval against Pakistan in 1954, taking 4 for 35 on a day that favoured swing bowling and in a team that included Statham and Loader. But Fazal Mahmood took 12 wickets and England suffered a stunning setback. In Brisbane for the first Test against Australia, he struggled to find his rhythm and Arthur Morris and Neil Harvey helped themselves to big centuries. Tyson was quick enough but after just 29 overs he had the galling figures of 1 for 160, bowling behind Bedser and Statham. England dropped 12 catches and lost by an innings.

Before the second Test began in Sydney Tyson cut down his run by 4 yards and, bowling with the wind at his back, took 4 for 45, including the wicket of Ray Lindwall who was sent ducking for cover from a bouncer. When it was Tyson's turn to bat, Lindwall bounced him and Tyson turned his head only to be hit squarely on the back of the skull. He was carried from the field with a lump visible from the boundary edge, but he came back to bat again and in the second innings took 6 for 85.

In Melbourne Australia needed 240 to win, but in front of 60,000 people who were expecting a close fight, they could only muster 111. Tyson took his best Test figures of 7 for 27 (6 for 16 off his last 51 balls) and a brilliant leg-side catch by Godfrey Evans to dismiss Harvey was the turning point. Australia lost their last eight wickets for 34 runs in an hour and 20 minutes!

England won the fourth Test at Adelaide to secure the Ashes, Tyson taking six wickets, and although the fifth Test was rained out, Hutton asked Tyson to bowl off just six paces to try for a result. The 'Typhoon' was still quick enough to knock the bat from the hands of Keith Miller. England had won the Ashes for the first time in Australia since Harold Larwood had caused similar chaos more than two decades earlier.

Bowling against Surrey on the normally docile Oval wicket in 1957, Tyson took 8 for 60, his best first-class figures, and followed up with 5 for 52 in the second innings. According to *Wisden*, nearly half the runs came from the edge of the bat.

Pitches at Northampton were not inclined to help pace in his day; Tyson's record of 509 wickets in the Championship and 766 overall was moderate and tends to add weight to the argument that his

NCE

inability to swing and control the ball scarcely put him in the upper bracket of the select fast bowlers. The very nature of his style posed an enormous physical strain and caused wear and tear and he was never destined to stay at the centre of the stage for long, yet while he was there, his impact was electric.

Derek Underwood

Born: 8 June 1945, Bromley, Kent

- His 45 not out at Headingley in 1968 remains the highest score by an England number 11 against Australia.
- The first eight-wicket analysis in England v Pakistan Tests came at Lord's in 1974 and included a spell of 6 for 2 from 51 balls.
- In 1976/7 he equalled Fred Trueman's England v India series record with 29 wickets.
- He took 100 wickets in a season ten times with a best of 157 in 1966.
- He was the leading bowler four times – 1966, 1967, 1978, 1979.
- At the age of 17 he was the youngest to take 100 wickets in a first season.
- He performed the hat trick for Kent v Sussex at Hove in 1977.

TEST CAREER	
BATTING	
M	86
I	116
NO	35
Runs	937
HSc	45*
Av	11.56
100	–
50	–
BOWLING	
Runs	7,674
Wkts	297
Av	25.83
Best	8-51
5w	17
10w	6
Ct	44
St	–

QUIET AND undemonstrative, with a shuffling gait, Derek Underwood enjoyed a career probably unique among English bowlers, although at first sight, he didn't look the type of cricketer to break records and upset traditions.

After a remarkable first season for Kent in 1963, when he became the youngest bowler ever to take 100 wickets, he took 9 for 28 the next year against Sussex at Hastings and 9 for 37 against Essex at Westcliff in 1966. He played in his first Test matches in 1966. Underwood's debut was against the West Indies at Trent Bridge where he did not take a wicket but bowled 43 overs for 86 runs in the second innings and batted with unexpected obstinacy to share in a last-wicket stand of 65 with Basil D'Oliveira.

His first official tour with the Under-25 side to Pakistan in 1966/7 was also not especially successful and it became the norm to regard him as a very good bowler in English conditions but ineffective on hard pitches overseas. He was not selected for the full tour to the West Indies a year later but went with a Commonwealth side to Pakistan and Sri Lanka where, after rain, he achieved the remarkable figures of 8 for 10 and 7 for 33 against the President's XI in Colombo.

Underwood's greatest triumph was to follow in 1968 in the last Test against Australia at The Oval. In the first innings he bowled 59.3 overs with customary steadiness and took 2 for 89 but on the last day there was a thunderstorm and when play became possible again only 75 minutes remained. If the wicket were to become difficult as it dried, then Underwood would clearly be the match-winner. Forty minutes passed before it did and then after one man fell to D'Oliveira Underwood took the last wickets in 27 balls to win the match with six minutes to spare, level the series and finish with figures of 7 for 50.

In the three-match series against New Zealand in 1969 he was in devastating form, taking 24 wickets

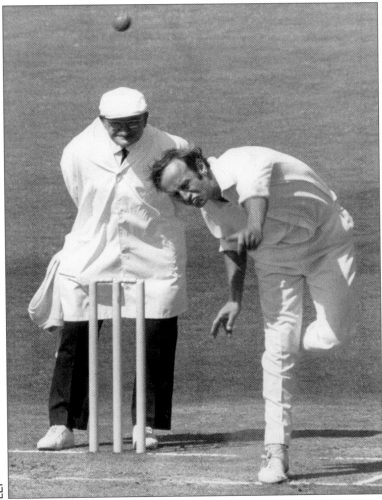

LEP

at 9.16 runs apiece. Though there were still those who doubted his effectiveness in Australia, he played an important part in the recovery of the Ashes in 1970/1, containing the Australian batsmen while the pace bowlers recovered and taking 16 wickets. At times the selectors overlooked him and in 1972 he was omitted until the fourth Test at Headingley where he returned match figures of 10 for 82. The match caused much controversy as a freak storm and subsequent strong sunshine led to a fungus removing the grass from the wicket, thus allowing spin from the start.

In the winter of 1974/5 he bowled steadily in Australia, coming into his own in the fifth Test at Adelaide when he had a damp patch to bowl into on the opening day and finished with 7 for 113. Against the all-conquering West Indians of 1976 he took the most wickets for England in the series – 17 – and a few months later on the successful tour of India his 29 wickets at 17.55 topped anything even the Indian spinners could achieve.

'Deadly' Derek was one of the English players who signed for World Series Cricket in 1977, wanting security for his wife and daughter. After Packer he seemed unsure of an automatic Test place despite taking his haul of Test wickets to 297. He decided to accept an invitation to join the 'rebel' tour of South Africa and was banned from Tests for three years. He was still bowling well enough to merit consideration in 1985 when the ban was lifted but the selectors ignored him.

Though he took 2,465 first-class wickets, perhaps his greatest pleasure came in 1984 when he scored his maiden century, 111 against Sussex at Hastings.

Cyril Washbrook

Born: 6 December 1914, Barrow, Blackburn, Lancashire
Died: 27 April 1999

- In Adelaide on the 1946/7 tour of Australia he shared in a third consecutive century opening partnership with Len Hutton.
- In Johannesburg in 1948/9 he shared in the then world record first-wicket stand of 359 with Len Hutton on the opening day of the second Test against South Africa.
- He scored seven double centuries, all for Lancashire, with a best of 251 not out against Surrey at Old Trafford in 1947.
- He exceeded 1,000 runs in a season 17 times (plus three on tour) and achieved a best of 2,662 in 1947.
- He scored 1,079 runs in the month of July 1946.

TEST CAREER

BATTING

M	37
I	66
NO	6
Runs	2,569
HSc	195
Av	42.81
100	6
50	12

BOWLING

Runs	33
Wkts	1
Av	3.00
Best	1-25
5w	–
10w	–
Ct	12
St	–

ALTHOUGH the Second World War arrived just as Cyril Washbrook was being discussed as a possible Test opener, he survived the hostilities with his batting form intact to become the Lancashire half of a renowned Roses opening partnership with Len Hutton.

Washbrook arrived at Old Trafford in 1933 aged 18. He played for a season or two with Ernest Tyldesley and for seven seasons with Eddie Paynter. The Lancashire coaches included Harry Makepeace, who taught him a great deal, and Cecil Parkin. A few weeks after his arrival at the club Washbrook played for Lancashire 2nd XI against Yorkshire 2nd XI and scored 202 not out – the first time the names Hutton and Washbrook appeared on the same scorecard. Washbrook was then promoted to the first team and scored 152 against Surrey in his second game. Four years later he received his first cap for England against New Zealand when Eddie Paynter, who had originally been picked to play, had to withdraw through injury.

During war service with the RAF Washbrook played all the cricket he could and in 1945 he took part in the so-called 'Victory Tests' which were staged in England at the end of the hostilities. He was picked for England in the Tests against India in 1946 and at Old Trafford on a difficult wicket he and Hutton showed something of their true mettle in a stand of 81. He was chosen to tour Australia and New Zealand in the winter of 1946/7. Hutton and Washbrook opened the England innings in all five Test matches, this series marking the beginning of their association as England's first-wicket pair. In the third Test at Melbourne Washbrook achieved a personal triumph, scoring 62 out of 179 in England's first innings and 112, his first Test century, in the second. At Adelaide the match was drawn though Washbrook and Hutton gave their finest performance as openers with two century partnerships. Their stands realised 137 and 100 exactly, Washbrook missing his own hundred by only half a dozen runs in the first innings.

Over the next season runs flowed prolifically from Washbrook's bat and his qualities as an opener with Hutton for England and with Place for Lancashire were acknowledged and admired wherever cricket was played.

Washbrook played in four of the five Tests against Australia in 1948, missing the match at The Oval through injury. He averaged 50.85 and scored more than any other England batsman except Compton. At Old Trafford he was 85 not out in England's second innings and looked well set for a century when a declaration was made in an abortive attempt to win the match. At Headingley he scored 143 in the first innings and 65 in the second, and he shared with Hutton in a century opening stand in each innings, a performance which established a new world record, for the feat had never been accomplished twice by the same batsmen.

MEN

Washbrook toured South Africa in 1948/9 and averaged 60.22. He and Hutton set up a new record for an opening partnership in the second Test at Johannesburg, their stand of 359 made in exhausting conditions on a hot day 6,000 feet above sea level. The fourth Test was played on the same ground and saw Washbrook fail by only three runs to make another hundred. He had hooked the previous ball for six, but in attempting to repeat the stroke, he was caught. After an unsuccessful tour of Australia in 1950/1 he was not selected again until 1956 when he was 42 years old. Persuaded to play in the Headingley Test against Australia, he joined Peter May with England 17 for 3. Between them, they decided the rubber, Washbrook having scored 98 vintage runs before succumbing inevitably to a forcing shot.

Lancashire's first professional captain, he served two spells as a Test selector and was President of his beloved red rose county.

Bob Willis

Born: 30 May 1949, Sunderland

- His 8 for 43 against Australia in 1981 is the best analysis in Tests at Headingley.
- At The Oval in 1981 he set a new England v Australia record when he passed the 109 wickets taken by Wilfred Rhodes.
- He became England's leading wicket-taker in the match against New Zealand at Wellington in 1983/4 when he exceeded Fred Trueman's 307-wicket record.
- He extended the world Test record for most 'not out' innings to 55 and the then record number of wickets by an England bowler to 325.
- He performed two hat tricks for Warwickshire, both at Edgbaston: v Derbyshire in 1972 and v the West Indians in 1976.

AFTER AN ERRATIC start in county and Test cricket Bob Willis, a gangling, rather open-chested fast bowler, developed into England's leading wicket-taker and appeared in more Test matches than any other fast bowler.

He made his debut for Surrey in 1969 but two years later joined Warwickshire because the presence of the established bowlers Geoff Arnold and Robin Jackman at Surrey made for limited opportunities. In 1972 he helped Warwickshire to their first County Championship in 21 years, taking 8 for 44, including the hat trick against Derbyshire at Edgbaston.

Early in his first-class career Surrey coach Arthur McIntyre tried to improve Willis's technique, believing he could turn the windmilling youngster into a fast bowler with a textbook action. But Willis's first delivery with his new style crashed into the side of the net and his confidence was shattered for weeks.

John Edrich convinced Willis to stay with the style that suited him best and two years later he flew

out to Australia as a replacement for the injured Alan Ward in the Test series which John Snow was winning. He played in four Tests, took 12 wickets at 27.41 runs apiece and thus began a long and rewarding association with the England Test team.

Willis was England's most aggressive bowler against the West Indians at home, on tour in 1973 and in 1974. In the lost Ashes series of 1974/5 he was England's fastest bowler. However, after that series he returned home for knee operations and many thought he would go the same way as the injury-prone Alan Ward. Thankfully he returned as quick as ever and on the normally dead wickets of India took 20 wickets at 16.75 apiece. At Bangalore, where Bedi and Chandrasekhar spun India to victory, Willis took 6 for 53 and at Calcutta his 5 for 27 helped England to a ten-wicket victory.

By 1977 Bob Willis was in peak form. He produced his best first-class figures: he achieved 8 for 32 for Warwickshire against Gloucestershire at Bristol and against the touring Australians took 27 wickets at 19.77 runs apiece, including 7 for 78 at Lord's.

LEP

LEP

Despite more knee surgery and an early return home from the West Indies in 1980/1, Willis reserved his greatest performance for Kim Hughes's Australians in a match in which Ian Botham's 149 allowed the home team a slender lead of 129 in the Headingley test. The Australians were cruising at 56 for 1 and Willis was looking like a spent force. He had come on as second change and had dropped in a number of no balls. He told Brearley that he could not bowl as he wanted to when he was charging uphill and into the wind, and pleaded for a shot at the Kirkstall Lane End.

On a pitch that was becoming more and more unreliable Willis got his way and his wickets. Aiming at cracks in the pitch just short of a length, he sent them down in one of the truly inspired spells of Test bowling. Throughout his career Willis's success had been based more on hard work than technique and his ability to fight adversity was never more evident than against the Australians. Willis finished with 8 for 43: Australia surrendered their last nine wickets for 55 and lost one of the most thrilling Test matches by 18 runs!

Willis was a surprising choice as England captain in 1982 and it was a role the Warwickshire paceman never seemed comfortable with. He was forced to relinquish the leadership to his deputy David Gower on several occasions because of injury and after winning seven of the 18 matches under his control, he eventually ceded the captaincy to Gower full time.

It is Bob Willis's all-out pace and determination, and of course that memorable day in 1981, for which he will be remembered.

Statistics

Selecting a best post-war England XI is a fascinating exercise but the results are bound to be highl provocative. Of course different players reached their best in different decades and comparisons can b odious. The more I thought about all the players who have represented England since 1946, the mor difficult the task of selecting my best XI became. How good a player is or has been is purely a matter o opinion, and it is certainly true that figures seldom tell the true story, but I hope the tables that appear on th following pages will go some way towards explaining why I have chosen the following players as my best XI o England's cricketers since 1946. I would like to point out that it wasn't easy to omit players of the calibre o Ken Barrington, Graham Gooch and Bob Willis.

1. Len Hutton
2. Geoff Boycott
3. Peter May
4. Denis Compton
5. Colin Cowdrey
6. Ian Botham
7. Alan Knott
8. Jim Laker
9. Fred Trueman
10. Derek Underwood
11. Brian Statham

TOP TENS

MOST MATCHES		MOST RUNS		MOST WICKETS		MOST CATCHES	
Graham Gooch	118	Graham Gooch	8,900	Ian Botham	383	Ian Botham	12
David Gower	117	David Gower	8,231	Bob Willis	325	Colin Cowdrey	12
Mike Atherton	115	Geoff Boycott	8,114	Fred Trueman	307	Graham Gooch	10
Alec Stewart	115	Mike Atherton	7,728	Derek Underwood	297	Graeme Hick	9
Colin Cowdrey	114	Colin Cowdrey	7,624	Brian Statham	252	Tony Greig	8
Geoff Boycott	108	Alec Stewart	7,469	Alec Bedser	236	Mike Atherton	8
Ian Botham	102	Len Hutton	6,971	Darren Gough	228	Graham Thorpe	8
Alan Knott	95	Ken Barrington	6,806	John Snow	202	Tom Graveney	8
Ken Barrington	82	Denis Compton	5,807	Andy Caddick	200	Allan Lamb	7
Mike Gatting	79	Ian Botham	5,200	Jim Laker	193	David Gower	7
Tom Graveney	79						
Len Hutton	79						
Allan Lamb	79						

BEST BATTING AVERAGE		BEST BOWLING AVERAGE	
Ken Barrington	58.67	Frank Tyson	18.5
Len Hutton	56.67	Jim Laker	21.2
Denis Compton	50.06	Fred Trueman	21.5
Ted Dexter	47.89	Brian Statham	24.8
Geoff Boycott	47.72	Alec Bedser	24.8
Peter May	46.77	Bob Willis	25.2
Dennis Amiss	46.30	Tony Lock	25.5
Tom Graveney	44.38	Derek Underwood	25.8
David Gower	44.25	John Snow	26.6
Colin Cowdrey	44.06	Angus Fraser	27.3

MOST HUNDREDS

Colin Cowdrey	22
Geoff Boycott	22
Ken Barrington	20
Graham Gooch	20
Len Hutton	19
David Gower	18
Denis Compton	17
Mike Atherton	16
Ian Botham	14
Alec Stewart	14

HIGHEST INDIVIDUAL SCORE

Len Hutton	364 v Australia at The Oval	1938
Graham Gooch	333 v India at Lord's	1990
John Edrich	310* v New Zealand at Headingley	1965
Peter May	285* v West Indies at Edgbaston	1957
Denis Compton	278 v Pakistan at Trent Bridge	1954
Dennis Amiss	262* v West Indies at Kingston	1973/4
Tom Graveney	258 v West Indies at Trent Bridge	1957
Ken Barrington	256 v Australia at Old Trafford	1964
Geoff Boycott	246* v India at Headingley	1967
Bill Edrich	219 v South Africa at Durban	1938/9

BEST BOWLING PERFORMANCE

Jim Laker	10 for 53 v Australia at Old Trafford	1956
Jim Laker	9 for 37 v Australia at Old Trafford	1956
Devon Malcolm	9 for 57 v South Africa at The Oval	1994
Fred Trueman	8 for 31 v India at Old Trafford	1952
Ian Botham	8 for 34 v Pakistan at Lord's	1978
Bob Willis	8 for 43 v Australia at Headingley	1981
Derek Underwood	8 for 51 v Pakistan at Lord's	1974
Angus Fraser	8 for 53 v West Indies at Port-of-Spain	1997/8
Angus Fraser	8 for 75 v West Indies at Bridgetown	1993/4
Tony Greig	8 for 86 v West Indies at Port-of-Spain	1973/4

WICKET-KEEPING

	Caught	Stumped	Total
Alan Knott	250	19	269
Alec Stewart	220	11	231
Godfrey Evans	173	46	219
Bob Taylor	167	7	174
Jack Russell	153	12	165

AVERAGES FOR ALL PLAYERS

	I	NO	Runs	HSc	Av	Runs	Wkts	Av	Best
Dennis Amiss	88	10	3,612	262*	46.30	—	—	—	—
Geoff Arnold	46	11	421	59	12.02	3,254	115	28.29	6-45
Mike Atherton	212	7	7,728	185*	37.69	302	2	151.00	1-20
Trevor Bailey	91	14	2,290	134*	29.74	3,856	132	29.21	7-34
Ken Barrington	131	15	6,806	256	58.67	1,300	29	44.82	3-4
Alec Bedser	71	15	714	79	12.75	5,876	236	24.89	7-44
Ian Botham	161	6	5,200	208	33.54	10,878	383	28.40	8-34
Geoff Boycott	193	23	8,114	246*	47.72	382	7	54.57	3-47
Mike Brearley	66	3	1,442	91	22.88	—	—	—	—
Chris Broad	44	2	1,661	162	39.54	4	0	—	—
Andy Caddick	81	9	773	49*	10.73	5,769	200	28.55	7-46
Brian Close	37	2	887	70	25.34	532	18	29.55	4-35
Denis Compton	131	15	5,807	278	50.06	1,410	25	56.40	5-70
Dominic Cork	53	8	781	59	17.35	3,647	124	29.41	7-43
Colin Cowdrey	188	15	7,624	182	44.06	104	0	—	—
Mike Denness	45	3	1,667	188	39.69	—	—	—	—
Ted Dexter	102	8	4,502	205	47.89	2,306	66	34.93	4-10
Graham Dilley	58	19	521	56	13.35	4,107	138	29.76	6-38
Basil D'Oliveira	70	8	2,484	158	40.06	1,859	47	39.55	3-46
Bill Edrich	63	2	2,440	219	40.00	1,693	41	41.29	4-68
John Edrich	127	9	5,138	310*	43.54	23	0	—	—
John Emburey	96	20	1,713	75	22.53	5,646	147	38.40	7-78
Godfrey Evans	133	14	2,439	104	20.49	—	—	—	—
Keith Fletcher	96	14	3,272	216	39.90	193	2	96.50	1-6
Angus Fraser	67	15	388	32	7.46	4,836	177	27.32	8-53
Mike Gatting	138	14	4,409	207	35.55	317	4	79.25	1-14
Graham Gooch	215	6	8,900	333	42.58	1,069	23	46.47	3-39
Darren Gough	83	18	806	65	12.40	6,288	228	27.57	6-42
David Gower	204	18	8,231	215	44.25	20	1	20.00	1-1
Tom Graveney	123	13	4,882	258	44.38	167	1	167.00	1-34
Tony Greig	93	4	3,599	148	40.43	4,541	141	32.20	8-86
Graeme Hick	114	6	3,383	178	31.32	1,306	23	56.78	4-126
Nasser Hussain	124	13	4,006	207	36.09	16	0	—	—
Len Hutton	138	15	6,971	364	56.67	232	3	77.33	1-2
Ray Illingworth	90	11	1,836	113	23.24	3,807	122	31.20	6-29
Alan Knott	149	15	4,389	135	32.75	—	—	—	—
Jim Laker	63	15	676	63	14.08	4,101	193	21.24	10-53
Allan Lamb	139	10	4,656	142	36.09	23	1	23.00	1-6
Tony Lock	63	9	742	89	13.74	4,451	174	25.58	7-35
Devon Malcolm	58	19	236	29	6.05	4,748	128	37.09	9-57
Peter May	106	9	4,537	285*	46.77	—	—	—	—
Chris Old	66	9	845	65	14.82	4,020	143	28.11	7-50
Geoff Pullar	49	4	1,974	175	43.86	37	1	37.00	1-1
Derek Randall	79	5	2,470	174	33.37	3	0	—	—
Tim Robinson	49	5	1,601	175	36.38	—	—	—	—
Jack Russell	86	16	1,897	128*	27.10	—	—	—	—
Mike Smith	78	6	2,278	121	31.63	128	1	128.00	1-10
Robin Smith	112	15	4,236	175	43.67	6	0	—	—
John Snow	71	14	772	73	13.54	5,387	202	26.66	7-40
Brian Statham	87	28	675	38	11.44	6,261	252	24.84	7-39
David Steele	16	0	673	106	42.06	39	2	19.50	1-1
Alec Stewart	207	17	7,469	190	39.31	13	0	—	—
Bob Taylor	83	12	1,156	97	16.28	6	0	—	—
Graham Thorpe	134	18	4,857	200*	41.87	37	0	—	—
Fred Titmus	76	11	1,449	84*	22.29	4,931	153	32.22	7-79
Fred Trueman	85	14	981	39*	13.81	6,625	307	21.57	8-31
Frank Tyson	24	3	230	37*	10.95	1,411	76	18.56	7-27
Derek Underwood	116	35	937	45*	11.56	7,674	297	25.83	8-51
Cyril Washbrook	66	6	2,569	195	42.81	33	1	33.00	1-25
Bob Willis	128	55	840	28*	11.50	8,190	325	25.20	8-43